A TREASURY OF NEWFOUNDLAND HUMOUR AND WIT

A
TREASURY OF
NEWFOUNDLAND
HUMOUR AND WIT

By
J. C. Burke
Illustrated: L. B. Jenson

BREAKWATER

©Copyright 1986 J.C. Burke

Reprinted in 1996, 2004, 2006, 2009, 2012

ISBN: 978-0-919519-97-8

 PRINTED IN CANADA

DEDICATION

This book is dedicated to Uncle Freeman Melbourne, whose own humour, love of life, and poetic turn of mind demonstrates what Newfoundland humour and wit is all about.

Uncle Free's "Phone Song," is ample proof that Newfoundlanders can write history and humour together because they see it as one and the same.

And to all those other Uncle Freemans whose humour, wit and wisdom gave us a rich and happy heritage, this book is dedicated.

FOREWORD

This little book of humour and wit is not a protest against the mainland "Newfie Joke," but a statement that we Newfoundlanders are better humourists than other Canadians. We can rightfully claim the coveted title of 'court jester' for the nation, the job of helping people laugh when laughter is the best medicine. And what is more important our humour, like all good humour, is at our own expense not someone else's.

Like the court jester in the days of our early kings it seems we are called upon to create laughter, relieve tensions, and, of course, to be an affectionate social critic. All of this must be done, like it was then, by reacting to fate, however comical, tragic or absurd with the confidence that he who can laugh at his own faults, foibles and follies will survive. Laughter becomes the 'safety valve' that helps us cope with the tragic and the comic in our existence and to transcend them.

Genuine Newfoundland humour, as Al Clouston has so ably demonstrated in his books, stems from the rich heritage that fate and circumstance bestowed upon us as a people. Isolation, hardships, uncertainties, and the adventure of living close to the sea have sharpened our wits and helped us to see the comic in the tragic and to laugh a hearty laugh and survive.

We have a lot to teach other Canadians through our humour. We can teach them how to cope with the uncertainties and difficulties of life by making use of the 'safety valve' of laughter.

Long ago when the future was not as bright with promise as it is today, we learned the secret of survival through laught   And it is hoped that when we share our humour and wit with the rest of Canada, that you, too, will be able to transcend the tragic and the comic for the moment and laugh with us to a healthier and happier state of mind and spirit.

J. C. B.

ACKNOWLEDGEMENTS

It is difficult to acknowledge all sources and originators of the stories and jokes that appear in this volume of humour and wit. Most of the stories were heard at banquets, church halls, and parties where people love to tell stories. Some of them can be rightfully attributed to the fun loving people of the happy province, the others are given a definite Newfoundland flavour, not so much because of the content, but by the Newfoundlander's unique way of telling a good story, and telling it with a flavour and taste that brings laughter rather than derision and ridicule.

We have some dandy story tellers in Newfoundland and some of the Newfoundlanders that have gone abroad have taken with them that inexpressible gift of being able to tell a good story. People like Dr. Cecil Webber, whose after dinner antics make you realize that the best things come after dessert; Uncle Freeman Melbourne, whose one liners are devastatingly funny; Bob Butler and Les Stoodley, whose absence from the rock makes the heart grow fonder and the stories funnier. And there were countless others who told me stories that appear in this book, or are kept on file for a second effort. Without your contributions this treasury of humour and wit would not have seen the light of day.

With acknowledgement to the father of Newfoundland humour and dialect, Al Clouston, I have written this volume, for the most part, in our second language, English. Next time around I might attempt a shot at the dialect. So "watch out, me son!"

Many people helped in the production of this volume. Apart from the people who provided the stories I am indebted to L. B. Jenson for his illustrations, Gordon MacLelland for his drawing on the front cover, Bob Butler for proof reading the material and Barbara Goodyear for typing the manuscript. And to my family who for the past several months have had to endure that first line, "Oh, did you hear this one?" Thank you for sharing this pleasurable task.

J. C. Burke

The Cabot Tower
St. John's

LBJ

1. WATCH OUT

The story is told of a gentleman in St. John's who lived on Long's Hill who called a watchmaker on Water Street to inquire how much it would cost to have his grandfather clock repaired. The watchmaker told him that repairs would cost ten dollars and that pick up and delivery would be five dollars each way. The old gentleman thought about it and decided that whereas it was down hill to the watchmakers he would take it down himself saving five dollars and have the clock delivered after repairs.

Despite the fact that it was the middle of February and a bit slippery underfoot, the old fellow strapped this huge eight foot clock to his back and proceeded cautiously in the direction of down town. Half way down Long's Hill despite his carefulness he lost his balance and was immediately swept away by the weight of the clock acting as a kind of toboggan over which he had no control.

To make matters worse at the foot of Long's Hill an old lady in her nineties was making her way gingerly across the street supported by two walking sticks and a pair of ice-creepers strapped to her fur-topped boots. Within an instant she was struck by the gentleman atop the eight foot grandfather clock and toppled into the nearest snowbank canes and all.

As he was struggling to his feet and adjusting the clock, he looked over in the direction of the old lady who by this time had brought herself to a sitting position on the snow bank. As soon as she got his attention she shook her fist in his direction and shouted, "why don't you wear a watch like everybody else?"

2. AN EXPURGATED EXPLANATION

An aging spinster was shocked at the language used by workmen repairing telephone wires near her home, so she wrote to the telephone company. The manager immediately asked the foreman on the job to make a report, which read as follows:

Dear Sir:

"Meself and George Williams were on this job. I was up the pole and accidentally let some hot lead fall on George. It struck him in the back of the neck and ran down his back. Then he looked up at me and said: "Really, Harry, you must be more careful!"

3. THOSE BIG ACCIDENTS

The story is told of two Newfoundlanders who went to Toronto to find work. When they arrived they were told by some friends that a large transport company was looking for a couple of long distance drivers for their California to Toronto haul. What was more interesting was the fact that both of them could be together on the one rig, as the long haul trucks allowed for one person to sleep for eight hours while the other person drove. This appealed to both of them and without hesitation they applied and were soon hired to take the job.

However, before going on the road they were obliged to take an intensive driving program to familiarize themselves with the vehicle. On one of the test runs the instructor said to the driver, "Tom, suppose your buddy was back there in the bunk asleep and you were coming down this long sloping hill, at the bottom of the hill a train was crossing the highway, you applied your brakes and the brakes failed, what would you do?"

"I'd call George," replied Tom.

"Why would you call George?" inquired the instructor.

"Because George haven't seen a big accident in his life." replied Tom.

4. BE YE PREPARED

A student at Memorial University who had failed in all his subjects wired his gentle mother as follows: "Failed in everything. Prepare father."

The mother wired back: "Father prepared. Prepare yourself."

5. READY FOR THE SECOND COAT

The oil money in Alberta had attracted Larry's attention to that province. Leaving his native Newfoundland behind he tried his best to fit into his new surroundings. Shortly after his arrival he dawned a new stetson, cowboy boots and a string tie, packing his rubber boots and bibbed cap away for when he went back home. His new duds helped in blending him into the Western lifestyle. However, he was still a little uncomfortable and not wanting to be branded an Easterner he decided that some lessons in horse back riding would certainly help. Soon he was taking lessons and out of the generosity of the stable owner was given the use of an old stable mare so that he could familiarize himself with the ways of this stately animal. He grew so attached to his horse that he rode it everywhere, especially to the small town bar where he liked to chat it up with his new friends and down a pint or two.

One evening when Larry was having a few drinks some of the boys at the bar, for a joke, painted his horse green. When Larry came out and saw what had happened he was fit to be tied. Half shot and mad as hell he staggered back into the bar and challenged whoever painted his horse to step up. A huge cowboy, standing some six and a half feet tall and weighing some two hundred and fifty pounds sauntered up to Larry and stated that he had painted the horse, and looking meaner than a rattle snake asked Larry, "and what are you going to do about it?"

Larry, assessing the no win situation, replied, "well, I just came back to tell you she's ready for the second coat."

6. NO VACANCY

There is a sobering reflection that stems from the story of George, the slow moving, ineffectual clerk in the small outport general store. One morning a villager entered and as was the custom of all the customers began calling for George. When no George appeared the villager turned to the owner, "George ain't sick is he?"

"No, not sick," said the owner, "just not working here any more."

"Is that so?" responded the curious villager. "Do you have anyone in mind to fill the vacancy?"

"No," said the owner again, "George didn't leave no vacancy."

7. FIGURING IT OUT

The Newfoundlander went into the office to apply for a job as investigator with the constabulary. The chief of investigations made him aware that perception was an important part of being a good investigator. The Chief making a figure two with his finger asked, "What is that?"

"I think it's a two," replied the Newfoundlander.

"Very good," said the chief. Making a letter H in the same manner he said, "What is this?"

"Looks like an H to me, sir," replied the Newfoundlander.

"Very good," said the chief. "Now I'm going to ask you a question but I want you to think about the answer. Who killed our Lord?"

"Well, sir," said the Newfoundlander, "you'll have to give me some time to figure that one out."

Leaving the office he met his friend, "say," he said, "I just got a job as an investigator with the constabulary, and I'm now on my first murder case."

8. AFTER THE INVESTIGATION

The story is told of the Newfoundlander who saw a well known Jew walking down Water Street. When the Jew approached he up and struck him on the chin knocking him back on the seat of his pants in the street.

"My dear man, why did you do that?" said the surprised Jew.

"Because you crucified our Lord", said the Newfoundlander.

"But that was 2000 years ago," he responded.

"Yes," said the Newfoundlander, "but I only found out about it yesterday."

9. NOT CONVINCING

Little Alex Smith had preached a scholarly sermon in which he set forth the proofs of the existence of God. At the close of the service he asked a kindly old saint, "and how did you like my sermon this morning?"

"It was a wonderful sermon, reverend," agreed the old fellow, "but in spite of all you said, I still believe there's a God."

10. SKEER EM!

The Newfoundland inventor arrived in St. John's to make arrangements to patent his newly invented mechanical scarecrow. The lawyer, somewhat skeptical, asked, "does it really scare the crows?"

"Skeer em!" he asserted, "why sir, that dere contraption skeered the crows so bad that some of em brought back seeds they'd stole two years ago."

11. INSTRUCTIONS

A traveling salesman held up in Flower's Cove on the Northern Peninsula by a bad snow storm, telegraphed to his firm in St. John's: "Marooned by storm. Wire instructions as of yesterday."

The reply came: "Start summer vacation."

12. DETERMINING THE DIFFERENCE

The oil firm put great stock in it's extensive intelligence tests. "Now what would you say is the difference between a little boy and a dwarf?" the personnel manager inquired of the prospective employee.

"Might be a lot of difference," said the prospect. "That particular dwarf," was the thoughtful reply, "might be a girl."

13. IF IT'S LOOKS YOU WANT

I knew a fish merchant who used to sell fresh fish near Woolworth's on Water Street some years ago. While picking up some fish one morning I happened to be behind a lady who himmed and hawed about the fish on display. She had almost decided on her purchase when she finally sniffed, "I really don't like the look of this mackerel."

"Ma'am," said the wary merchant, with what patience he had left, "if it's looks you want, why don't you go into Woolworth's and buy a goldfish?"

14. A STRAIGHT ANSWER

The story is told of a long distance transport driver from Newfoundland who enjoyed knitting on his treks to Toronto and back. One day when he was driving through Nova Scotia a police officer was shocked to see the driver of this huge transport with his arms through the steering wheel knitting at about the same speed the truck was travelling.

He gave chase and with some difficulty came up alongside the transport truck and began to signal it to stop. The driver, busy with his knitting and all, did not notice the police car so the cop came alongside the rig and shouted to the driver, "pull over!" "pull over!"

The driver of the truck on seeing the cop replied, "no sir, it's a cardigan."

15. BEYOND A MOTHER'S LOVE

The local merchant was going over his books when he noticed that one delinquent customer had failed to pay his bills. In the customary fashion the merchant sent this reminder:

"In looking over our accounts we find that we have done more for you than your poor mother. We have carried you for eighteen months."

16. READ CAREFULLY

The gentleman with a pair of glasses in need of minor repairs dropped in at a store featuring the sign, "Glasses Repaired While You Wait."

"You can call for these on Tuesday," he was told.

"But," protested the gentleman, "how about your sign, "Repairs While You Wait?"

"Well," said the shopkeeper, with unanswerable logic, "you'll be waiting, won't you?"

17. LACKING THE ESSENTIALS

The two friends had come over to sit with widow Jones whose husband, a sea captain, was drowned at sea.

"My, o my," said one, "tis a shame that skipper George met such an uncertain end."

"Yes it was," commented the other, "but I hear you'll get two hundred thousand dollars in insurance. Is that right?"

"Yes it is," said the wife.

"Imagine that," said the first, "and the poor man couldn't even read nor write."

"Nor swim," added the wife.

18. NEXT TIME SEND INSTRUCTIONS

After the Second World War the government was offering a variety of assistance programs to veterans in an effort to re-establish them in the work world. One such program for veterans was assistance in establishing small agricultural farms and small businesses. The story is told about one veteran who wrote the agricultural department for assistance in establishing a poultry farm. He indicated that he had ample space, some thousands of square feet, and could probably handle 3000 chickens to start with.

The agricultural department sent the veteran the 3000 day-old chickens. However, three weeks later he sent for an additional 3000 chickens, and three weeks after that another request came for another 3000 chicks. The agricultural department thought it strange that the veteran was requesting so many chickens so quickly although he appeared to have sufficient space, so they sent a representative to call on the newly established farmer.

When the rep arrived he saw no buildings, only a large area of newly broken ground. Approaching the veteran farmer he asked, "How are you doing with the chicken farm?"

"Not very good," the farmer replied, "I don't know if I'm planting them too deep or too far apart."

19. RISKING A REPUTATION

The owner of the new restaurant was sampling the soup by the newly hired cook.

"You say you served overseas?" said the owner.

"Yes, sir," said the cook, "I was officer's mess cook for two years and I was wounded twice."

"You're lucky," the owner replied, after sampling another spoonful of soup, "it's a wonder they didn't kill you."

20. A COUPLE MORE

"That's a hard working little wife you have," remarked a friend.

"She's that alright," replied the proud husband, "I wish I had a couple more just like her."

21. REACHING A COMPROMISE

Local road work was one of the 'make work' projects that the provincial government carried out annually in every outport community that did not have its own town council.

A grant of money would be allocated and the men of the community would work for a few days, working one day for wages and the next day for free. The men didn't put a great deal of effort in the road work, especially the days when they worked for the government. One old fellow was telling me that one of the men went up to the foreman one day and announced, "Skipper, the shovels haven't arrived yet. What will we do?"

The foreman said, "ah, tell the boys they'll have to lean on each other until they get here."

The old S.S. "Bruce" 1913 —
Linking Canada with Newfoundland

LBJ

21

22. CHECKIN' ON MESELF

Jobs were, and still are, hard to find in Newfoundland. If you got a job you were considered lucky and you did your best to hang onto it. One young man who acquired a job as a handyman to one of the St. John's merchants walked into a downtown store and asked to use the telephone. He placed the following call:

"Is dat you Mr. Ayre? — Well, Mr. Ayre, did you want a handyman around your place? — "Yes, sir. . . . You say you already got a handyman workin' for you? . . . Is that right? . . . Well, are you satisfied with him? . . . Then you ain't thinking of making a change? . . . Thank you, sir."

He hung up the receiver and thanked the clerk for the use of the phone. She, having overheard the conversation, mentioned that if he was looking for a job there was a vacancy at the store, pointing to the sign in the window saying, "Help Wanted."

"I'm not looking for a job," said the young man. "I already have a job. I've been working now for three months."

"I don't understand," said the clerk somewhat puzzled. "Why were you calling up that gentleman?"

"Oh, that's the man I'm workin' fer. I was just checkin' up on meself."

23. JUST ONCE

The wife of the visiting clergy sat alone in the congregation while her husband occupied the pulpit. At the close of the service an usher greeted her, not knowing her identity. "Do come again," he urged, "and don't think we have such poor preaching regularly. That man is here for this service only."

24. ALL THE REST IS PROFIT

Local merchants in Newfoundland possessed the ingenuity to make a success of an enterprise despite a subsistence economy. Starting with little or no capital and little or no formal education most made a success of merchandising in the little towns and villages on the island. Even today businesses are still run successfully by people who had little or no formal business education. Those who have a formal business education are not particularly welcomed by the old guard merchants even if they happen to be relatives. As is illustrated by the story of the young MBA who accepted a position in the retail business that his father had conducted with considerable success for forty years.

The young man, however, was not satisfied with his father's business practice. "We should take an inventory," he said, "or how will we know what we have made?"

"Son," said the father, "see that bolt of denim on the shelf over there? Measure it and see what it's worth."

"What will that tell you?" the young graduate demanded.

"Mostly everything. I started with a bolt of overall material just like that. All the rest of the place is profit."

25. THE AILMENT

The workman on the hydro dam had been reading over a sheet of technical instructions. "What's a cubic foot?" he asked the foreman.

"I'm not quite sure," was the reply. "Go in and ask the superintendent, he'll know."

The superintendent was puzzled but helpful. "You go ahead and make up a claim," he said, "and I'll make sure you get full compensation."

26. TO TELL THE TRUTH

A politician running for office was very much incensed at certain remarks that had been made about him by the town's leading newspaper. He burst into the editorial room and accosted the editor.

"See here," he declared angrily, "you are telling lies about me in your paper and you know it."

"Well, that's nothing to get upset about," retorted the editor calmly. "Just suppose we told the truth about you?"

27. DIPLOMACY

The wood's crew had nominated the meekest man in camp to interview the tough foreman and register a complaint about the food.

"Don't like the grub, eh," growled the foreman. "What's wrong with it? Not enough of it?"

"Oh, no, sir," assured the complainant. "There's plenty of it, such as it is."

"So, it's not good enough for you, eh?"

"Oh, yes, it's very good, what there is of it."

Ferryland — here in 1623
Lord Baltimore established his First Colony

I.B.J.

24

28. NARE BIT OF LARNIN'

Malcolm arrived in North Sydney and within six hours had landed himself a job as janitor of Wesley United Church. This was right up his alley, close to home and working in familiar surroundings, as back home he seldom missed a church service. Things were going well until one morning one of the leading ladies of the Church called. The minister was out at the time so Malcolm answered the phone. "Good Marnin ," says Malcolm, "what can I do fer 'e?" The lady, taken aback somewhat asked for the Minister. Malcolm advised that he wasn't in but that he would take a message. The lady stated that she had an announcement for the Sunday bulletin and asked Malcolm if he would write down the details for the Minister. Malcolm sadly replied, "my dear, I can't read nor write. You see I was barn up the bay where there was no school, so I got nare bit of larnin'." The lady thanked him politely and hung up.

Later that week she called and complained bitterly to the Minister regarding the new janitor and insisted that Malcolm, because of his poor English and lack of education, be replaced. The Minister was obliged to tell Malcolm that at the end of the month he had to go, giving as his reason that the church required a janitor who could act as backup for the clergy when he was away.

So Malcolm, like most Newfoundlanders, headed for the New Jerusalem, Toronto, where he figured his lack of education would be less of a hinderance than it was in North Sydney.

Arriving in Toronto, he was as equally quick to pick up a job on construction, and next day began work on one of the city's tallest buildings. For one year Malcolm worked hard, made suggestions, and endeared himself to his fellow workers and management. He was proud that he was a part, even though a small part, of such a large project.

One day, however, nearing the completion of the building the foreman came to Malcolm and told him the executive director of the company wanted to see him. Malcolm, a little apprehensive, went to the large oval office and presented himself to the top man. "Malcolm," said the gentleman, "I want to personally congratulate you on your many suggestions to management in the construction of our building. You have saved us more than a quarter of a million dollars in overall costs. That, in our estimation, is terrific. However, what I want to propose to you at this time is the possibility of you taking over the leasing and management of the whole complex. We have every confidence that you can do it. What do you say?"

Malcolm replied, "I'm sorry sir, I can't do it. I got no larnin'. I never went the school in me life. I can't read nor write."

"You can't read or write?" replied the surprised executive. "My dear man, what would you have done and what would you have been if you could read or write?"

"I would have been the janitor of Wesley United Church in North Sydney, sir." replied Malcolm.

29. ONE FOR THE MINISTER

The visiting minister apologized for the brevity of his sermon. He explained that just before he left home, his dog chewed up and destroyed most of his sermon notes. At the close of the service a parishioner whispered to the guest preacher: "If that dog of yours ever has any pups, I wish you would give our minister one."

30. HOW MUCH MORE?

With confederation came many benefits to the Tenth province. However, there also arrived undesirables who sought to make a quick buck on the island by defrauding the innocent citizens. One such person was caught and brought before the magistrate for a hearing, found guilty, and was about to be sentenced. The magistrate, a person of a benevolent aspect, fixed his mild blue eyes upon the defendant. "Prisoner at the bar," he said, "you have been convicted of a serious crime. It now devolves upon this court to fix a punishment. If you have anything to say in your own behalf — anything that will help ease the penalty for your crime — this is the opportunity."

"Well, your Honour," said the criminal, and his manner was quite jaunty, "you probably know how it is yourself. The more a fellow has in this world the more he wants."

"Is that so?" said the magistrate. "Well, sir, I'm going to give you ten years in Dorchester. How much more would you like to have?"

31. KNOW MORE

The judge was getting ready to hear the case before the Supreme Court, and to clear the final matter he asked the defendant, "sir, do you know any members of the jury?"

Defendant: "Some, your Honour."

Judge: "Do you know more than half of them?"

Defendant: "Your Honour, I'd say I know more than all of them put together."

32. ITS THE MUSTACHE

"As soon as I saw you coming around the curve," said the officer, "I said to myself, 'fifty-five at least'."

"Well, you're way off on that one, sir," said the driver, "it's the mustache that makes me look so old."

33. TRIED

The local magistrate was discussing beverages with a friend, "Have you ever tried gin and haig ale?" asked the friend.

"No," replied the magistrate, "but I've tried a lot of folks who have."

34. ONLY GOD KNOWS

The magistrate had just sentenced Old Charlie to three months on Salmonaire Line, despite Old Charlie's protest of innocence. As the police officer was taking him out of the courtroom, Old Charlie muttered something under his breath which caused the magistrate to order him back before the bar.

"What do you mean," demanded the now irate magistrate, "by using profane language in connection with this court? How dare you curse me: I am strongly tempted to add an extra six months to your sentence."

"Judge," pleaded Old Charlie, "I didn't say nothin' agin you."

"Have you the face to stand there and tell me that a minute ago, as you were being led from this room, you did not mutter under your breath profane utterances aimed at the dignity of this court?"

"No sir," stated Old Charlie, "Judge, lemme explain. I just got to thinkin' dat even if I ain't got no justice in dis world I'll certainly be able to explain when I gets to Heaven how come I got snarled up in this mess. So I begins talkin' to meself. I just says, God am the Judge, God am the Judge, God am the Judge! . . . jus like dat, sir."

35. MEETING THE CHALLENGE

"Now, sir," said the judge to the prisoner, "if you wish, you may challenge any member of the jury."

"Well, sir, I'm not in the best of condition, but I believe I can lick that little feller at the end of the front row."

36. FIGHTING MAD

The young feller was in court on a charge of fighting. "What is your side of the story?" asked the Judge.

"I was in the telephone booth talking to me girlfriend when the other fellow came along and wanted to use the phone, so he opened the door, grabbed me collar and threw me out of the booth."

"And that made you angry enough to start a fight?" asked the Judge.

"No, your honor," was the reply, "I didn't get fighting mad until he grabbed me girlfriend and threw her out, too."

37. WHOSE STILL MADE THE MOONSHINE?

The song "The Moonshine Can" attests to the fact that the making of a little moonshine was not an uncommon practice in some quarters of our fair island. Some, as the song relates, were caught and if we can call it justice saw their various contraptions confiscated and a price paid for instilling the forbidden spirits.

Very often when the magistrate came to hold court such cases as "moonshining" could bring about an amusing exchange of good Newfoundland banter and wit. Such was the case when a Moonshiner named Joshua was brought before the magistrate in one of the outports. The magistrate noting the defendant's name and having a fair knowledge of the good book began, "Joshua, Joshua, you wouldn't be the Joshua that made the sun stand still?"

"No sir," replied the defendant, "I'm the Joshua whose still made the moonshine."

38. ACQUITTED

In Christmases past in Newfoundland every home was opened to friends and strangers alike. People came from far and near to mummer, or just to visit for a drink or some syrup and cake. Very seldom would there be cause for disagreement or the lodging of complaints against those who came in the spirit of the season. However, there was one case where a Christmas reveller came to visit and after he had left it was discovered that a Christmas gift, a Newfoundland tartan shirt, was missing from under the tree.

The gentleman, a member of the community was approached about the matter, but denied that he had stolen the shirt. However, the family felt the matter was grave enough to take the gentleman to the local magistrate in the hope of having the shirt returned.

The trial was set and the case was heard before the court. The magistrate in summing up the case concluded that there was insufficient evidence to find the defendant guilty of stealing the shirt, and that he considered the case closed and the man acquitted. Whereupon the defendant inquired, "acquitted? Your Honour does that mean I can wear the shirt now?"

39. A NEAT GIFT

You heard about the Newfoundlander who went to the lumber yard in Toronto and asked to have a box made 100 feet long by 1 inch by 1 inch. The gentleman at the yard thought that this was an odd order and inquired as to why he wanted a box of such strange dimensions.

"Well," said the Newfoundlander, "I'd like to giftwrap a clothesline I bought for my mother for Christmas."

40. I'LL TEACH HIM MYSELF

Little Georgie had picked up quite a vocabulary of cuss words. His mother, shocked and perturbed, questioned him as to where he could have learned such words. Georgie replied, "I learned them at school." So the anxious mother sat down to write to Georgie's teacher. She began very gently but as the enormity of the offense struck her she concluded, "If all Georgie learns in school is to swear, I'll keep him home and teach him myself."

41. SOME ENDEARING QUALITIES

The doctor came into the kitchen and said to Mrs. Rielly, "I don't like the look of your husband."

"Neither do I, sir," she replied, "but he's good to the children."

Mount Moriah, Bay of Islands
West Coast

LJ

42. TELLING IT LIKE IT IS

"Doctor", said the patient, "if there is anything wrong with me, don't frighten me half to death by giving it a scientific name. Just tell it like it is. Give it to me in plain English."

"Well, to be frank with you," replied the doctor, "you're just plain lazy."

"Thank you, doctor," said the patient with relief, "now give me a scientific name for it so I can go home and tell the missus."

43. THE MILESTONE

Uncle Mose was celebrating his one hundredth birthday and was being interviewed by one of the local newspapers. After several questions about eating habits, exercise and philosophy, the reporter asked, "and to what do you attribute the fact that you have reached this remarkable milestone?"

"Well," smiled the old man, "I dare say I'd have to say that the main reason I got to be a hundred years old was that I was born in 1880."

44. THE NEW MATH

The teacher was teaching arithmetic to a class of youngsters.

"If a boy by himself could pick six quarts of berries in an hour and a girl could pick five quarts, how many quarts would they pick together?"

"Teacher," said an overgrown youth from the back, "I don't know exactly how many, but it wouldn't be eleven."

45. KEEPING UP

A few years ago it was not uncommon for a neighbour or several neighbours for that matter to come over and spend an evening yarnin'. It was understood that come a certain hour the guests would leave and let the folks go to bed. Sometimes the hint that you may have overstayed was subtle indeed as was the case with the fellow who said, "I really must be going. I hope I haven't kept you folks out of bed."

That's all right bye," came the response, "we would have been getting up soon anyway."

46. THE LECTURE

A fellow was telling me about the drunk who was going home one morning when he was stopped by the local constabulary.

"What are you doing on the streets at 4:00 o'clock in the morning?" the cop demanded.

"Going to a lecture," he replied.

"At 4:00 a.m.?" was the derisive reply. "Do you expect us to believe that?"

"You would sir," sighed the man, "if you knew my wife."

47. LACKING TACT

The young couple in the small outport village had their first baby. It was a beautiful child but strangely enough it had no ears. The young couple, despite this obvious deformity, doted upon the child and were proud parents indeed. In fact the whole community was happy for the couple, and despite the fact that small villages are given to gossip and talk, no one mentioned that the child had no ears, and everyone accepted the child as a normal healthy little fellow that he was.

One day a relative arrived back from Toronto to visit his parents and soon after his arrival mentioned that he would like to go over and visit the young couple and their new baby. The mother cautioned him not to mention the fact that the baby had no ears because the parents were sensitive about it, and further, it wasn't good manners to bring it up. He assured his mother that he would not mention anything about the child's ears and off he went to pay the couple a visit.

Arriving at their home he greeted them and asked how everyone was. He congratulated them on having a new son and proceeded as is the custom to make something of the baby.

"He's a fine little fellow," said the visitor, "does he keep well?"

"Oh yes," said the father, "he is a perfectly healthy child."

"His eyesight is good I suppose?" went on the visitor.

"Yes," replied the father, "the Doctor said he's got 20-20 vision."

"O that's good," commented the tactless one, "because he'll never be able to wear glasses."

48. CAN'T KEEP THE WINNINGS

Mike was approached by one of his buddies. "Mike," he said, "we are counting on you to buy a ticket for the raffle we're arranging for the penniless widow Sullivan."

"You can stop countin'," said Mike, "even if I did win her the wife wouldn't let me keep her."

49. APPRECIATING THE OFFER

"You finally asked father for my hand!" exclaimed the young lady. "What did he say?"

"Not a word," the young man replied, "he just fell on my neck and sobbed."

50. MORE THAN A MAN CAN TAKE

Two elderly spinster sisters were sitting at home enjoying a quiet evening. Suddenly one of the sisters looked up from her paper and commented: "There's an article here telling of the death of a woman's third husband in Toronto. She has had all three of them cremated."

"Isn't that life for you?" said the other, "some of us can't even get one husband, while that bunch on the mainland have husbands to burn."

51. THE COMFORTS OF HOME

The travelling salesman walked into the small outport restaurant one morning and told the waitress, "Bring me two eggs fried so hard they are edged in black, two slices of burnt toast and a cup of cold coffee. Then sit down and nag me, I'm homesick."

52. EFFICIENCY

The efficiency expert from the mainland was hired to cut down on waste, and to speed up production. He arrived at the plant and began his analysis of the work situation. He was not more than a couple of hours into his appointed task when he came upon a spectacle which shocked his efficient being to the core.

On a bench sat a lanky, languid looking fellow chewing tobacco. He would, every once in awhile, bend forward and spit, but apart from that he was totally immobile.

Figuring he had come upon at least one reason for the plant's inefficiency, he approached the gentleman and began his inquiry.

"Sir", he began, "what do you think you're doing?"

"Me?" inquired the other, "I ain't doin' nothin'."

"Well what do you expect to do when you get through doing nothing?" asked the expert.

"Nothin much," said the fellow on the bench.

"How long have you been sitting here doing nothing?" the expert demanded.

"Oh, bout an hour — maybe an hour and a half," said the man, leaning foward to spit again.

"Is that so? How much do you draw a week?" he asked.

"Oh, bout seventy-five dollars," the man on the bench stated.

"When is your week up?" asked the expert.

"Tomorrow in fact," he replied.

"You needn't wait until tomorrow — you can go right now. Here!" The efficiency expert reached his hand into his pocket, hauled out his own private roll of bills, peeled off seventy-five dollars and handed it to the chap on the bench saying, "Now get out of here and don't ever let me see you inside this plant again."

"Yes, sir," said the loafer, and got up, spat a farewell, and slouched off.

"I guess that's inaguarating a little rough and ready reform right at the start," said the efficiency expert to himself. He called the foreman and when he arrived he asked, "who is that fellow walking out of the gate?"

"I don't rightly know his name, sir," said the foreman. "But he's got some kind of a job at the United Nail and Foundry Company up the street."

53. A BIRD'S EYE VIEW

Most Newfoundlanders were told when they were small that they came from cabbage stumps. So when the idea of a stork bringing babies began to replace other more traditional explanations some questions were raised. Take, for example, the little fellow who had just been told that the stork had brought him a baby sister. "Would you like to see her?" asked the doctor.

"Nope," said the boy, "but I'd sure like to have a look at that stork."

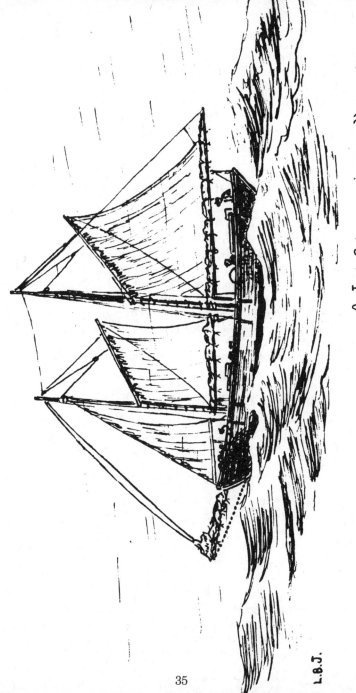

A Jack Schooner in squally weather

L.B.J.

54. AS YOU LIKE IT

The young lad had gone to spend the weekend with his mother at a friend's house. When bedtime came, the mother discovered that she had forgotten to pack her son's pajamas.

The lady of the house suggested that little Albert use one of her daughter's nighties seeing they were about the same size.

However, Albert protested bitterly, "I won't put on a little girl's nightie," he proclaimed, "I won't sleep in a little girl's nightie. I'd rather go to bed raw."

55. ROUNDING OUT THE TALLY

Newfoundland families up until recently were quite large. It was not unusual for a couple to have a dozen or more children, and in many cases the families numbered in the twenties.

Mrs. Carr, a lady of Irish descent wanted to keep her family on the small side. Shortly after her twelfth child arrived she was out hanging a line of clothes when a neighbour happened along and congratulated her on the new arrival. Having a whimsical turn of mind, the good neighbour greeted the woman with, "well, I heard the good news, 'tis quite a string of little carrs ye have now, Ma'am."

To which Mrs. Carr replied, "yes, but the last one was the caboose."

56. LOOKS ARE NOT EVERYTHING

The young fellow proposed to the girl, "Will you marry me?"

"Well," she said, "I will, but I'm not very good looking."

"Ah, that's all right," he said, "you'll be out to work all day."

57. GETTING THE FACTS

The census man came to collect the vital statistics from the family. Speaking to the man of the house he said, "Is this your wife?"

"Why sure it tis," he said, "you don't think I'd be living in sin with an old hag like that do ya?"

58. THE LAST WORD

The Church anniversary service was about to begin. The guest preacher and other visiting dignitaries were gathered in the vestry. The radio crew flitted about making sure that the broadcast would go without a hitch. Everyone had received instructions and were given time limits on their parts in the service so that the program would end on the hour.

The service had begun and things were working according to schedule until the guest preacher got into his sermon. He had been allotted twenty minutes to deliver the anniversary address, but when the twenty minutes were up he was still in mid-flight, and, ignoring all signals to stop continued with his oratory. In desperation the church's pastor tried to get his attention, and failing decided to toss the Red Hymn Book in his direction with the hope that the slight commotion would bring the visiting preacher back to the realization that his time was up and that he should stop.

Unfortunately the Hymn Book sailed past the pulpit and struck an old gentleman in the front pew square between the eyes. As the old fellow was passing into a state of unconsciousness he was heard to say, "hit me again I can still hear him. Hit me again I can still hear him."

59. HERE TODAY AND GONE THE SAME DAY

The Bishop had come to the little outport church for confirmation services. It was a beautiful summer's day and a fine cooling breeze blew off the water through the open windows into the neat little white church perched on the hill.

The Bishop unmindful of the strength of the breeze laid his sermon notes on the pulpit and commenced prayers. The breeze lifted the notes and took them through the open window and scattered them around the village. On returning to the pulpit to give his address to the people he was disturbed to find his notes missing, but having a ready wit and making the most of the situation he said to the congregation, "My dear people when I came here this morning only God and I knew what I was going to say to you . Now only God knows."

Another clergy who found himself in the same predicament found a comforting thought in the words, "The Lord gave and the Lord has taken away. Blessed be the name of the Lord."

60. CONSIDERATION

A minister who suffered extremely strained relations with his congregation was finally appointed chaplain at the Provincial Prison in St. John's. Elated to be rid of him so easily, the people came in great numbers to hear his farewell discourse. The minister planned to have the last word so he chose as his text, "I go and prepare a place for you . . . that where I am, there ye may be also." (John 14:3)

61. QUICK REPARTEE

In the outports of Newfoundland the minister was, and still is, one of the most respected citizens of the community. And if he were single he would probably be the most sought after eligible bachelor by the young women of his congregation. At one time to marry a minister was a sign of God's favour indeed. And many a young minister had to try and avoid the plots and traps of young and not so young ladies. The story is told of a young bachelor minister who arrived in this small community to take up his appointment in July. It happened that a young widow of the congregation felt that he would make a fine second husband, so she set about to win his affections. Later that week she invited him over for afternoon tea. They sat in the living room making small talk when she suggested that they go into the back garden and sit under the tree in the shade. It was an unusually warm and sunny day with a light breeze blowing through the trees. Sitting under the tree you could hear the birds singing, the bees buzzing, and the whole scene was calm and peaceful.

Having what she felt made a good beginning she searched her mind for something romantic to say and having lit upon a phrase she turned to the unsuspecting clergy with a romantic glint in her eye and said, "Reverend, do you hear the wind moaning and groaning through the tree?" Whereupon the young parson looked up at the tree for a moment and turning to his lady companion replied, "Yes, and if you were as full of green apples as this tree you'd moan and groan too."

62. SUGGESTIONS

"Are you the game warden?" asked the lady over the telephone.

"Yes, I am the game warden," came the reply.

"Oh, I am so glad," she said, "could you please suggest some games for a little party we are having at the church social?"

63. LET'S BE REASONABLE

Tom and Dick were partners in a retail coal business before the dawn of the oil stove. Business was good and the two seemed to be doing alright.

One fall a revivalist came to the community and Tom met the Lord and got converted. In his new found glory Tom tried to persuade Dick to join the Church and give his heart to the Lord. "Why," he asked, "don't you join the church like I did?"

"I think it's a fine thing for you to belong to the church," replied Dick with some reasoning, "but if I join, who'll weigh the coal?"

64. A DEALS A DEAL

Dr. Cecil Webber tells the story of the couple who came to the minister to get married some years ago. Not having any ready cash they offered to pay the minister in kind, so the promise was made to have a quintal of dried fish landed at the parsonage as a fee for the minister. This, of course, was not uncommon in those days as the barter system was the prevailing means of exchange.

When the wedding was over the clergyman mindful of his fee said to the groom, "I trust that the quintal of fish will be of good quality."

The groom, with a twinkle in his eye, replied, "now Parson, you'll have to take that fish like I took the missus, for better or for worse."

65. THE WOES OF BEING DOUBLE-JOINTED

Bob Butler tells this story about his dad, the Rev. W. R. Butler who preached in Newfoundland. One Sunday the Rev. Butler had a young theological student visit his parish, and as was the custom, the young man was invited to preach at the morning service. In contrast to the Rev. Butler's sometimes lengthy discourses, the young man was short and to the point, which delighted the young people of the congregation and was well received by others.

Feeling a little threatened by the favourable comments the younger man's sermon was receiving at the dinner table that day, Rev. Butler embarked upon an impressive critical analysis of the young preacher's message. However, the younger members of the family were not to be intimidated by their father's learned remarks, and in a less learned manner insisted that the young man had done an excellent job and, to their delight, in good time. Mr. Butler realizing that he was in a no-win situation, not as much from their logic, as from the fact that he was outnumbered sought to close the conversation with the face saving comment, "well, all I am saying is that I thought that the sermon was a bit disjointed."

Whereupon one of his children responded, "well, dad, all we are saying is that it was a lot better than some of the double-jointed ones we've heard."

66. GETTING THE ANSWER FIRST

The minister in the Church in the small outport pastoral charge was loved and respected by his congregation but his salary was necessarily small. When the opportunity came to accept a call to a much larger city church with considerable raise in salary he was torn between the loyalty of his flock and the enticement of the new offer.

"I suppose," mourned one member of the flock to the preacher's son, "your father will accept the call to that big city congregation?"

"I dunno," admitted the boy, "dad's on his knees in the study at this very moment praying for guidance."

"And your Ma?"

"She's upstairs packing the trunks."

67. SERVE THE LORD WITH GLADNESS

One of the exciting events of the year in the small communities along the South Coast was to have his Grace the Lord Bishop of the Anglican Church visit the communities for services of confirmation. And in places where there was no rectory the honor fell on some worthy member of the congregation to provide accommodations for his Lordship during his stay in the community. This was a great honour, and those who were chosen went all out to make the Bishop's stay a pleasant and memorable one.

Mr. and Mrs. Jones had just had word that the Bishop had graciously accepted their invitation to spend the weekend as a guest under their humble roof. The weekend came, he arrived and was welcomed. He was now sitting down to his first meal at the Jones' table. Mrs. Jones rushed about and encouraged the good Bishop to eat heartily. Mr. Jones, swollen with a sense of honor, began or ended every sentence with the gracious word 'Lord'.

As a special privilege, little Georgie, aged five, had been permitted to sit at the table with the Bishop on condition that he be on his best behaviour and refrain from speaking unless first spoken to. Mindful of his pledge the little fellow sat in silence, his eyes fixed upon the face and form of the good Bishop.

However, a spontaneous sense of hospitality moved him to break the promise when he saw the Bishop's eyes roam up and down the well spread table as though seeking for something.

"Ma!" said Georgie, "oh, Ma!"

"What is it, Georgie?" asked his mother.

"God wants a pickle."

68. KNOW THY OWN

The Newfoundlander went to see the Anglican clergyman with a rather strange request. "My pet Budgie has died and I was wondering if I could get permission to bury it in the cemetary?"

"A Budgie in an Anglican cemetary?" repeated the clergy, "certainly not!"

The man said, "well, if I went to the United Church up the road, do you think that they would let me bury it in their cemetary if I gave them a thousand dollars?"

The clergy said, "a thousand dollars? You should have told me that it was an Anglican Budgie."

69. A CASE OF MISTAKEN IDENTITY

The story is told of an old lady in one of the outport communities who was bedridden for a number of years. She enjoyed visitors and because of a failing memory often mistook people for someone else.

One day the minister came to visit and as it was the case with every visitor, the daughter brought the guests to her room and introduced them. In introducing the minister she indicated to the old lady that he was the "new minister." The old lady with not a clear recollection asked if he had not been their earlier in the week and that she may have already met him. The daughter replied that the young man who visited earlier in the week was the doctor who came to examine her.

"Why, of course," replied the old lady, "I thought he made himself a little too familiar to be the clergyman."

A hamlet on the southwest coast

LBJ

70. THE LORD WILL PROVIDE

In the local parishes in outport Newfoundland finding enough funds to meet the needs of the church was always a critical problem. In this one congregation the Session of the church had before them a critical issue. They were informed that they could secure some much needed hymn books for use in the Church from a pill company, if they permitted the company to carry a small advertisement on the inside cover of each book. The debate raged for hours until it was finally concluded that the offer of the hymn books not be accepted on the basis that the church could not accept hymn books that carried pill advertising.

A letter was sent to the company thanking them for their kind offer and expressing their reason for declining. However, a few weeks later a package arrived at the post office for the parish. It contained a sufficient quantity of hymn books and upon examination no advertising appeared on the inside covers. The congregation was delighted with the gift and everyone was more than happy that at last the much needed hymn books were supplied.

However, all went well until Christmas when the minister announced one of the congregation's favourite Christmas carols. It was this particular carol that the advertisers chose to put in their plug for the pills. The carol read,

> Hark! the herald angels sing,
> Beecham's Pills are just the thing,
> Peace on earth, and mercy mild,
> Two for a man, and one for a child.

71. SELF CONTROL

The clergyman was playing a game of golf with a gentleman who was addicted to profanity. At every bad stroke — and there were many such — the latter cut loose, poisoning the air with unseemly cuss words. The reverend was also off his game but he said not a word, merely locking his lips together tighter and tighter.

At the 10th hole the layman went all to pieces. Following the ninth stroke, as his ball soared out of one bunker to pass over the green and descend in another bunker on the far side, he flung down his club, danced in the sandpit and spouted forth his entire profane vocabulary. When comparative calm had returned to him he turned to his clergy companion and asked, "George, with all due respect to your profession, I don't see how you do it. Tell me how is it humanly possible even for a minister of the gospel to keep from swearing on a golf course once in a while anyway?"

"My friend," said the clergy, "when I finally reached the stage where I simply cannot contain myself any longer, I turn my head and I spit. And where I spit the grass never grows again."

72. THE ANSWER

"In time of trial," said the visiting minister, "what brings us the greatest comfort?"

From the rear of the church came the answer, "an acquittal."

73. JUST THIS LITTLE PROBLEM

Someone was telling me that a few years ago in Port aux Basque Dr. Samuel Baggs was preaching one of his usual forty minute jobs when a gentleman sitting near the front got up in the middle of the sermon and left the church.

The next day Dr. Baggs, assuming the man was unwell, and this being the reason for his leaving the church in the middle of his sermon, paid the family a visit. When he arrived he met the wife at the door. "Good afternoon," said Dr. Baggs, "I came over to see how your husband was, I noticed that during my sermon yesterday morning he came out of the church."

"Bless your heart," replied the wife, "he's fine, sir, he's just got this little problem that sometimes he walks in his sleep."

74. TOO LATE

The minister had overlooked an elderly parishioner in handing out invitations to a garden party he and his wife had planned for the back garden. Thinking of her at the last minute he called, "I'm sorry, Mrs. Jones, we just forgot to ask you to come to today's garden party. Please accept this late invitation."

Mrs. Jones replied, "it's too late, I've already prayed for rain."

75. IN THE SERVICES

In almost every village on the island you will find in their little churches marble plaques with a list of those who have given their lives for their country. In Newfoundland the war dead are often referred to as those who had died in the services.

One morning a father had come to the church with his young

son, and while in the porch the young boy asked his father what was written on the marble plaques. The father said, "those are the names of the men who died in the service".

To which the child replied, "which service, dad, the 11 or the 7 o'clock service?"

76. WHAT'S IN A NAME?

A clergy was visiting a Newfoundland family one afternoon and was surprised to learn that despite the large number of children everyone in the house, including the parents and grandparents had a biblical name. He was so taken with the thought that he made it the subject of his conversation, and learned from the old gentleman that not only did every person in the house have a biblical name, but that the dog lying near the stove was named after a dog in the New Testament. This really aroused the clergyman's interest. However it puzzled him as to what the dog's name might be. He could not, in all his studies, recall a dog mentioned by name in the the New Testament. Whereupon the old chap set out to instruct the clergyman as to where he got the name for his dog.

"Sir," he said, "do you mind the story of the Rich Man and Lazarus in the Bible?"

'Yes, indeed," said the still perplexed clergy.

"Well that's where we got the name for our dog. We called him after the one in that story. It says right in the Bible, 'and moreover the dog came and licked his sores.' So his name is 'Moreover.'"

77. JUST LIKE SANTA CLAUS

Now speaking about the Devil. Two little girls were coming from Sunday School discussing what they had learned.

"Do you believe there is a devil?" asked one.

"Of course not," replied the other promptly. "It's just like Santa Claus. He's your father."

78. NOT IN A POSITION

When it became apparent that Patrick O'Flanigan's life was ebbing away fast, Father MacGrath was called to administer the last rites. "Pat", said the priest, "you've given me a lot of trouble in your lifetime, but I realize that you are a good man at heart.

Now that you are about to die, are you ready to accept God and renounce the Devil?

Pat thought this over in silence for a while. "Father," he finally said, "I'm certainly willing to accept God, but at this particular time I don't feel I'm in a position to antagonize anyone."

79. WHAT CAN I DO FOR 'E?

You better learn to like Newfoundlanders because you might meet them in unexpected places. If this story is true be real nice to them.

There was this fellow who hated Newfoundlanders. He died and arriving at the Pearly Gates he knocked and heard a voice from inside answering, "well me son, what can I do fer 'e?"

80. NOT THE RIGHT CROWD

The evangelist was holding forth at the prayer meeting. He had just outlined the conditions for going to heaven. To make sure that everyone got the message he asked whoever wanted to go to heaven to stand up.

Nearly everyone stood up except a gentleman in the front and an old lady sitting in a seat behind him. Turning to the old lady the gentleman said, "Martha, don't you want to go to heaven?"

"Not if that bunch is going there, I don't," she replied.

81. GETTING IN

Into posh Timothy Eaton United Church walked this Newfoundlander. After making some inquiries, and facing some difficulty, he located one of the the ministers and said, "Sir, I'd like to join this church. We used to get Mr. Eaton's catalogues all the time back home, and now it would be nice to go to his church.

The minister was appreciative but asked, "my good man where do you live?"

"I live across town," replied the eager worshipper.

"Then don't you think it would be wise to join a church in your own neighbourhood?"

"Yes sir, but I desires to join this church," said the man.

The minister pondered, "My good man," said he, "suppose you go home and pray over this important step."

The man agreed. The next day he appeared. "Reverend," he said, "I went home and did what you told me. When I asked the

Good Lord how I could get into Timothy Eaton Church he said: 'George, why do you ask me how to get into Timothy Eaton? Why, man, for the past ten years I've been tryin' to get in that church myself."

82. EXCEPT WET

Every year in my hometown of Victoria in August or thereabouts the Pentecostals would hold their baptismal service at Beaver Pond, and the whole community, whether you were a Pentecostal or not, would gather to witness the annual baptism of new converts.

On one occasion I recall a very powerful evangelist who before the actual baptism took place addressed the crowd something as follows, "my brothers and sisters in the Lord, hark to my words. It isn't good enough that you should have words of thanksgiving on your lips, or that you be shouting 'hallelujahs' and 'amens'. No, unless you got the spirit of the Lord pressing heavy upon you and the old time religion in your soul; unless you have happy hopes of the hereafter and the fear of Satan; unless you have all these feelings, you won't get nothing when you get immersed in the water — except wet."

83. MODERN CONVENIENCES

Going to Toronto to find work has been a tradition with Newfoundlanders for years now. Earlier it was to Boston or some other New England location. However, most of those who were obliged to leave their native land always dreamt of coming back home someday and settling down. Some do return and bring with them the treasures of their experience. There is the story of the young man who came back from Toronto to his little outport village, and on his arrival home he set about to improve and modernize his father's house.

He suggested that a bathroom be installed and that a patio be built on the back so that the family could cook and eat outdoors. This seemed to turn the old man's world upside down. "You mean to say, that we're going to eat outdoors and do what we do outdoors in the house? My son, we can't do that," complained the old man.

"Yes we can, father," reasoned the son, and he went about to install the bathroom and build the patio.

A few weeks passed and the bathroom was finally ready, but

by this time the old man decided that he wasn't going to use it. He would, for his part, continue to use the outdoor toilet as he always did. To solve this problem the son decided that the outhouse had to go and in the quickest possible way.

A day or so later he was going down the road when he stopped to talk to the construction crew that was building a connector highway to the community. He related his problem and one of the chaps suggested that he take a stick of dynamite and a cap and blow up the old outhouse, especially since it was a comfortable distance from the other buildings. The demolition expert on the road crew offered both the stick of dynamite and his expertise to solve the problem. "An excellent idea," was the immediate response. So they went up to the old outhouse, planted the dynamite and placed the cap. Lighting the fuse they hid behind some large boulders a safe distance away. Shocked they were when peeping over the boulders they saw the old fellow entering the outhouse. Their warning shouts did not penetrate the old man's deafness and he went inside. About 30 seconds later there was an explosion and the old chap with trousers wrapped around his ankles from the blast and the back missing from his shirt was catapulted into the air and landed in the tall grass at the bottom of the garden. The young man, white with fright, rushed to pick his father up. Arriving where he was lying in the grass he took his father's head in his lap and looking down into his face pleaded, "father, father, are you alright? Are you alright?"

The father managed a weak reply, "yes, son, I'm alright, but just imagine if I had done that in the house."

84. THIS ISN'T BULL

The Shepperds of Shepperdsville, a small community just east of the Baie Verte turn-off on the Trans-Canada highway, have some of the largest families in Canada. Some eleven families in the early seventies represented over ninety children. With such large families you could expect some ribbing. So it was when one of the Shepperds decided to take the family to Silverside one fall to the agricultural fair. Visiting the different booths and attractions the clan came upon the showing of a prize bull that required admission. Going up to the wicket the father ordered "two adults and thirteen children's tickets please." The young man in the booth looked out on the throng with some consternation and then asked, "Are all these yours?"

To which the father replied in the affirmative.

"Then," said the young man, "you stay here and I'll bring the bull out to see you."

85. IT WAS THE STORK

Having that many children requires that you also have a sense of humour. Someone was telling me that when Allan's wife was having her tenth child he sent for the doctor in Springdale to attend her. The doctor obliged and drove to Shepperdsville in the middle of the night to assist in the delivery. When he turned into Shepperdsville from the Trans-Canada he nearly ran over what appeared to him to be one of Allan's ducks waddling across the road. Arriving he said to Allan, "I nearly killed your duck a minute ago coming up the road."

Allan replied, "Doctor, I don't have any ducks."

"Well," said the doctor, "it looked like a duck to me."

"Ah doctor," said Allan with a grin, "that musta been the stork with her legs wore down."

86. WHAT A FUSS

In Newfoundland not so many years ago a common dessert on Sunday for the evening meal was Jelly and prunes, or blanc mange and prunes. This dessert was popular because of its availability and affordability. The prunes also had a medicinal value, so for years the Ex-lax trade was non-existent in Newfoundland.

Not everyone, however, enjoyed their prunes and jelly, but for the most part people were happy to get a dessert at all and most ate their little dish of dessert and were thankful. Young Sammy was an exception. Having had prunes for supper he was coaxed to eat all but two, but there he stopped and no amount of coaxing could induce him to go farther. Finally, as a clinching argument, his mother explained that God would be very angry if he didn't eat the remaining two prunes. But Sammy remained unmoved. Triumphant, if disgraced, he was marched off to bed.

Later that evening a terrific storm broke out, and fearful that the erring boy would be terrified, his mother crept into the darkened room. There was young Sammy standing at the window untroubled by the thunderous fury without. Between the crashes of thunder the mother heard him speaking and, forgetting her own nervousness, she tip-toed up behind him. He was muttering in disgust, "What a fuss — over two old prunes."

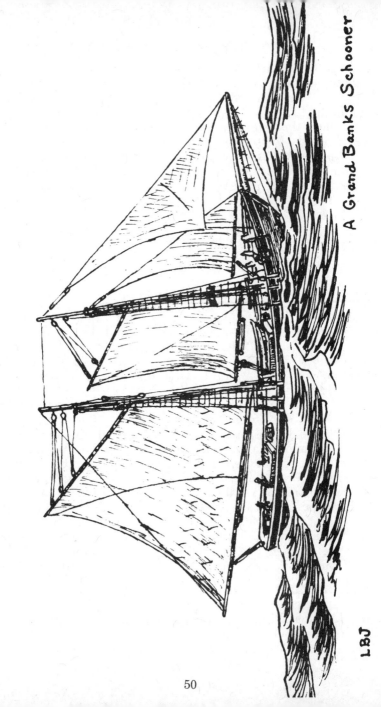

A Grand Banks Schooner

LBJ

87. A BETTER LIFE

Sometimes finding the right words to express your feelings can be difficult. This was not the case with John. John, not having too much of the world's goods, nevertheless loved the good things of life. So when an uncle, who was old and stingy died and left him a sizable sum John advised his relatives and friends of the good and bad news in these words,

"Yesterday, at five in the morning, my uncle and I passed on to a better life."

88. I DID IT MY WAY

The story is told of an interesting old codger who used to live in one of the small fishing villages on the South Coast. He was a boat-builder by trade — made dories, skiffs and smacks as good as anyone on the island. Occasionally he was called upon to build a pine box for anyone who died in the community.

One day, so the story goes, another resident of the village fell grievously ill. Friends who had gathered realized the sick man could last only a few hours longer, so a couple of them went to see the old boat builder at his shop and asked if he would make a coffin of a suitable size and have it ready when the bereavement actually occurred.

The old fellow balked. It seemed he didn't like the neighbour who was dying. And even under the circumstances he refused to forget the grudge. Despite the pleading on the part of the delegation that came to see him he refused to stop what he was doing to make the coffin for the man.

The delegation withdrew to consult further. After exhausting all arguments and unable to come up with someone else to build the coffin they were at their wits end. Then one of the group had an inspiration. He went home and soon returned with a large bottle of Newfie Screech and, going to the shop, presented the rum to the old fellow with his compliments, and once more renewed the request that he fill the order designed for the future use of the man with whom he had had the feud.

Well, a drop of rum can go a long way in straightening out petty feuds, and in this case the old chap listened to reason, accepted the peace offering, and agreed to build the coffin.

Working alone behind locked doors the neighbours could hear the old fellow using hammer, plane and saw. About dusk all sounds ceased.

A couple of the men went up to the boat-house door and knocked. There was no answer. So they forced an entrance. Inside they found the old fellow lying asleep on a pile of shavings in the corner of the shed. Alongside him was the 40 ouncer — empty. But on two work horses in the middle of the boat-house stood the completed coffin, lid and all. There was just one unusual feature. It had a rudder on it!

89. ALL VISIBLE SIGNS OF WELCOME

The gentleman dropped in to the veterinarian hospital in Corner Brook and asked: "I wonder if you fellers could remove my dog's tail?"

The vet, somewhat puzzled, asked, "why do you want your dog's tail removed?"

"Well," said the man, "my mother-in-law is coming to visit us and I want to eliminate all visible signs of welcome."

90. TAKE NO CHANCES

The Newfoundlander whose mother-in-law had died suddenly in Halifax was faced with a critical decision. The telegram that announced the sad news asked for instructions, "Should we bury her or cremate her?"

After a moment's thought the Newfoundlander cabled back, "Both, take no chances."

91. THE VALUE OF THE DOLLAR

The old lady went to the hospital to see her husband who was just getting over an operation. On her arrival back from her visit she commented to one of the relatives that her husband looked some bad, — "I wouldn't give two cents for him tonight," she remarked.

"He's pretty nigh dead then," replied Uncle Charlie, "especially if that two cents is reckoned on the Canadian dollar."

92. A MATTER OF CHOICE

"Well George," said Angus, "I hear you up and got married?"
"Yes Angus, I did," said George.
"And what kind of a wife did you get? Can she cook?"
"No. I don't think she's much of a cook."

"Can she sew?"

"No bye."

"Then what can she do, old man?"

"I'll tell you what, she's a great singer," replied George.

"Your crazy, me son," said Angus, "wouldn't a canary been cheaper?"

93. WIFELY DEVOTION

In Newfoundland it is not uncommon to see demonstrated in the quiet little homes tangible evidence of wifely devotion. Newfoundland women have always played an important role in family life, and have given unstintingly of their time and energies to husband and children. So it was with Martha, who not only drew the admiration of her family, but also friends and neighbours. One evening two acquaintances were discussing this same matter of devotion when one remarked, "now take Martha, she certainly thinks a lot of her husband."

"Now how would you know that?" inquired the other.

"Well," said the first, "what do you feel about a woman who really believes that the parrot taught her husband to swear?"

94. THE CAMPAIGN TRAIL

Joey Smallwood is well loved in all parts of Canada. In Newfoundland he is still considered the most astute and wittiest politician that the island ever produced. The following little incident that was purported to have happened to him on the campaign trail demonstrates the kind of wit that was uniquely Joey's.

In the crowded Hall in Twillingate Joey was waxing eloquent in urging the voters to get out and vote, and to vote for him, when a man in the rear of the hall jumped to his feet and shouted. "I'd rather vote for the devil!"

"That's your choice," rejoined Joey, "but should your friend decline to run, can I count on your support?"

On another occasion Joey was campaigning when a homely looking woman approached him and shouted, "why Mr. Smallwood, I wouldn't vote for you if you were Saint Peter himself."

To which Joey responded smilingly, "if I were Saint Peter Madam, you wouldn't be in my constituency."

Ah Joey we like you when you're witty but we don't like you when you're half-witty.

95. A TERSE REPLY

Talking about chicken farming, everyone in the outports usually kept a few hens in the back yard for eggs. The story is told of one old lady who had some trouble with her flock and wrote the Department of Agriculture the following letter:

Dear sir,

There is something amiss with my hens. Every morning I find two or three lying on the ground cold and stiff with their feet in the air. Can you tell me what is the matter?

After about three months she received an official reply from the Department of Agriculture:

Dear Madam,

Your chickens are dead.

96. IF ITS ALRIGHT WITH THE UNDERTAKER

Political patronage in Newfoundland, while it created scandals, also had its lighter moments. The story is told of a perennial office seeker who upon learning that an important government official had just died hurried to Mr. Smallwood's office to tell him that he'd like to "take the deceased man's place."

Mr. Smallwood replied, "if it's alright with the undertaker, it's alright with me."

97. A PERSONAL VIEW

The guest at the hotel had just left the manager's office, where he had entertained complaints about the service, the rooms, the meals, the prices, and even the weather. As he passed the newsstand the girl behind the counter called out cheerfully, "would you like a magazine, sir?"

"No, thank you," was the quick reply.

Undaunted the girl tried again. "How about some nice postcards with views of the hotel?"

"Thank you," said the man, "but I have my own views of this hotel."

A Mug-up on the Humber
(from Capt. Kennedy)

L.B.J.

98. AT THE BOARDING HOUSE

The boarders had gathered for the evening meal at the boarding house in St. John's. The landlady had supplied, along with other things, a platter of very thinly sliced cold cuts.

One of the boarders, a witty bayman asked the lady very politely, "did you cut these?"

"Yes, I did," came the reply.

"Good," he said, lifting the platter, "then I'll deal."

99. SUSPICION FOUNDED

"I'm suspicious of that fellow in room 108," the hotel manager told the security guard. "You'd better go up and have a look around."

When the security guard came back downstairs the manager asked, "did you find any of our towels in his suitcase?"

"No," answered the guard, "but I found your chambermaid in his grip."

100. A BREAKFAST SONG

The boarder was pleased to hear the landlady, as she prepared breakfast, singing the hymn, "Nearer, My God, to Thee."

At the breakfast table he told her that he was pleased to have found a place where there was a bit of religion and someone who could start the day in such a fine frame of mind.

"Thank you, sir," she replied, "that's the hymn I boil the eggs by — five verses for hard, and three for soft."

101. BOARDING HOUSE LOGIC

All Newfoundlanders who have had the experience of staying in the typical St. John's boarding house will appreciate this bit of logic that was rendered to three young lodgers who had violated the regulations of the house.

After being out to the wee hours of the morning and causing a ruckus when they did arrive, they were confronted the next morning by the gentleman of the house who said,

"A fine pair you three. Didn't get home last night until this marnin'. If you want to stay here yor're going to have to get out."

102. TIPPING YOUR HAND

The Newfoundlander accompanied some friends to the rather posh restaurant where the menu was printed in French and the atmosphere high class. Not wanting to show any sign of ignorance or lack of acquaintance with the reading of a menu in French, he took it in his hands and studied it with an air of great intentness. Then pointing his finger at a certain item near the top of the menu he said to the waiter who was waiting for his order, "to start off with, I'll take some of that."

"I'm sorry, sir," said the waiter, "but the orchestra is playing that right now."

103. THOSE BLOWOUTS

The first automobile was being unloaded off the ferry at Port aux Basque. Standing on the wharf were a number of curious onlookers who were eager to see their first motor car.

When the driver got into the vehicle one of the young men came over to him and asked, "Can this thing go very fast?"

"Yes sir," came the reply, "It can travel up to fifty miles an hour."

The young man all decked out in his rubber boots and bibbed cap figured the mainlander was putting him on, and suggested that he could run as fast as that thing could go. The driver responded by saying, "well if you want to take me on for a race, I'll accept the challenge." So away they went.

The driver starting off in low gear maintained a slow fifteen mile an hour pace for the first mile and the Newfoundlander ran with ease alongside. He stepped it up to 30 miles an hour and still the Newfoundlander kept pace. Stepping it up to 50 miles an hour he figured he would lose sight of his fleet footed competitor, but was surprised to find that he was maintaining close range despite the fact that he looked winded and his tongue was hanging out.

After taking a sharp turn in the road he looked back and discovered the Newfoundlander was no longer trailing the car. He turned and went back and just as he was rounding the turn again he saw the Newfoundlander emerging from the alders by the side of the road. He was badly lacerated and his clothes were torn and tattered.

The driver asked, "what happened? You were giving me a run for my money before this happened."

"Yes," replied the Newfoundlander, "and I would have passed you on the stretch if I hadn't got a blow out in me long rubber."

104. WITH OR WITHOUT

George and Harry were out in the cabbage garden when Harry looked up into the sky and seeing the silver flash of a jet and its stream of exhaust against the sky said to George, "I wouldn't want to be up dere in she."

To which George replied, "I wouldn't want to be up dere without she."

105. TROUBLES

Engine trouble forced an airplane pilot to bail out over Newfoundland. On his way down he was surprised to see floating through the clouds an old lady.

"Hey", he shouted. "did you see a plane going down?"

"No, my son," replied the old lady, "but did you see an oil stove going up?"

106. A COD'S HEAD FOR THE CAT

This fellow came down on the stagehead where the men were gutting the fish. "Have you got a cod's head for the cat?" he asked.

"What do you want a cod's head for the cat for?" said one of the fellows. "Are you doing a transplant?"

107. STOP PRESS

The following news item appeared in the local paper: 'The body of a woman believed murdered 500 years ago was discovered by archaelogists in the Port aux Choix area. The R.C.M.P. are now looking for a 542 year old man who may be able to assist them with their investigation.'

108. THE IMPOSSIBLE DREAM

The Newfoundlander was standing outside in the yard when a high flying bird struck him on the head with some droppings. The lady of the house noticed this and appreciating the man's predicament said, "I'll run into the house and get you some toilet paper."

"It's no use," he replied, "by the time you get back with it that bird will be a mile away."

Arctic Ice in Harbour
— St. John's

L.B.J.

59

109. SPECIAL ATTENTION

The chap said to the waiter, "excuse me, but do you have pig's feet?"

"Yes I do," he replied.

"Tell me then," he said, "where do you buy your shoes?"

110. LET'S DO IT MY WAY

This Newfoundlander went for his driving test. The examiner came out and sat in the car with him. "Any questions before we start?" asked the examiner.

"Will it be OK if I drive around in me long rubbers?" asked the Newfoundlander.

The examiner replied, "let's try it with the car first."

111. BILINGUALISM

Mr. Clarke and Mr. Parsons had been separated for a number of years. Now these childhood friends in their middle age were reunited again. Mr. Clarke had come home from Halifax, N.S., on his first visit to his old hometown and Mr. Parsons who had eked out a living fishing with his father was more than glad to see his childhood buddie.

After they renewed their acquaintance Mr. Parsons introduced his wife and twelve year old son, Isaac. Mr. Clarke felt that he ought to make a lot of the boy, knowing the father was proud of his offspring.

"A fine boy" he said with some feeling, "and bright looking too! Is he good in school?"

"He's a good student," explained the proud father. "He's good in all his subjects but he's some smart with langwidges. Come on Ikie say 'horse' in Algebra for Mr. Clarke."

112. QUITE A DIFFERENCE

The young college student had just arrived back from Memorial University where he had got his first introduction to anthropology — the study of man. He was anxious to demonstrate his advanced thinking to the more conservative members of the community so he sauntered down on the wharf where some of the old salts from the village were yarnin'. He struck up a conversation, and during the course of it suggested that man was descended from the apes. Citing Charles Darwin and his Origin of Species, he figured he clenched the argument. "I can't see," he went on, "what difference it would make to me if, say, my distant grandfather had been an ape."

To which an old sage, sucking on his pipe and looking wistfully out to sea, replied, "no Martin, perhaps it might'n make a big difference to you, but it might have made quite a difference to your grandmother."

113. PARTICIPATION

Orientation week at Memorial was always hard on Freshmen. The initiation into the institution of higher learning often put one's life in danger to say nothing of what might happen to the innocent and unsuspecting public. One year, however, things had gone too far. One frosh was nearly drowned in Quidi Vide Lake and after her ordeal she reported the incident to the dean who undertook an investigation.

One of the first to be summoned before him was a youth who owned up that he had participated in the incident in question.

"Ah ha!," snarled the dean, "you confess, then, that this inoffensive youth was carried by force to the lake and there immersed?"

"Yes, sir," said the young man.

"And what part did you take in this disgraceful affair?"

"The right leg, sir."

114. MISTAKEN IDENTITY

Two Newfoundlanders who had been in a celebrative mood met in St. John's. The strong smell of Newfie screech was evident on their breath as they settled into a congenially hiccoughy conversation.

"Seems like to me old feller, I've seen 'e somewhere afore," said one of the gentlemen.

"I wouldn't be surprised," said the other, as he made an effort to maintain his balance.

"Didn't I meet you one time in Corner Brook?"

"Not me. I was never in Corner Brook."

"Come to think of it," slurred the other, "neither was I."

"Well then, the question is, who the hell was those two fellers that met in Corner Brook?"

115. WHEN ALL ELSE FAILS

The story is told of a little girl who was a resident of an orphanage in St. John's. The superintendent there decided that her mentality was defective. She lagged behind other children of her age in her studies. So she was turned over to the Waterford Bridge Hospital for the mentally ill.

On her arrival at the hospital the little girl was given extensive tests and placed under expert observation. As a result, the head physician decided that she was merely subnormal and accordingly she was returned to the orphanage. The day after she returned, two of the other children were discussing her.

"Did you hear what happened to Francis?" said one of them.

"No — what?" asked the second.

"You know she was sent away to be an idiot, don't you?"

"Yes."

"Well, she couldn't pass and had to come back."

116. MISSING THE MARK

The party was just getting into full swing. Everyone had already sampled the Newfie Screech and the home-brew. The local musicians had taken up their instruments and were making the old rafters vibrate with a medley of Newfoundland songs, jigs and reels.

In the corner a gentleman who was brought to the party by one of the friends of the hostess sat with his head in his hands, and when the music stopped, burst into loud sobs.

The hostess noticing this hurried over to the man and putting her hand upon his shoulder said, "you must be homesick, that the music should make you cry like this."

He raised his tear-stained face, "no ma'am," he replied, "I'm a musician."

117. A SECOND CHOICE

A rather disliked outport doctor whose competence was drawn into question came one evening to visit a patient who was ailing for some time. "I feel," said the doctor, "that you're the kind of person who wants to know the facts. You're a very sick man. Is there anyone in particular you would like to see?"

The doctor leaned down to catch the feeble answer. "Yes, doctor, there is."

"And who is it?" asked the doctor.

Came the reply in a much stronger tone, "another doctor."

118. GETTING AWAY

The Newfoundlander was telling a friend of his narrow escape in France during the Second World War. "The bullet went in me chest and came out me back," he said.

"But," protested his friend, "it would have gone through your heart and killed you."

"No, me son," said the veteran, "me heart was in me mouth at the time."

119. AFTER DUE CONSIDERATION

The sailor was shipwrecked and after spending five years on a deserted island, was overjoyed to see a ship drop anchor just offshore. A small boat was launched and in a short time an officer from the ship landed and handed him a bunch of Evening Telegrams.

"The captain suggests," he told the sailor, "that you read what's going on in the world and then let us know if you want to be rescued."

120. HELPFUL HINTS

The lady taking the St. John Ambulance course arrived at the meeting in a state of great excitement. "I have just had the opportunity," she said, "to apply the knowledge we have acquired here in our first aid class. I had just crossed Water Street when I heard a terrible crash. A man had been hit by a car. I hurried over. He had a compound fracture of the tibia. He was unconscious, and was bleeding profusely from scalp lacerations. It was terrible, but my St. John's Ambulance training came in handy. I leaned down and put my head between my legs and prevented myself from fainting."

121. SOMETHING LACKING

A Conne River resident was in Grand Falls giving blood at the Red Cross blood donor clinic when another donor, during the rest period, recognizing him to be of Indian descent asked curiously, "Now would you really be a full-blooded Indian?"

The Conne River man considered the question for a moment, then he responded, "I was," he said, "now pint short."

122. THE SPARE PART ANTIQUE

The antique collector was looking over the household effects just before the sale. "That looks like a mighty old axe," he remarked.

"Sure is," said the old timer, "been in the family more than a hundred years."

"Remarkable," said the collector, "you've certainly taken good care of it."

"We've done that," agreed the old fellow, "even in my time it's had four new handles and three new heads."

123. ON THE RIGHT TRACK

The couple who had spent all their days out around the Bay moved to St. John's. On their first day in their new surroundings the old lady said to the Skipper, "I suppose it's about time you was up and made on a fire".

"Well now, missus," he says, "why don't we start right off using the city conveniences. Call the fire department."

124. A QUICK REPLACEMENT

Tis wit that makes the Newfoundlander a man apart. I recall hearing a story of two brothers who were constructing a new wharf on their stagehead. One of the brothers picked up a large piece of timber and commenced to put it in place when the other brother noticed that the piece of timber was worm-eaten and not too sound.

"I wouldn't use that piece of timber, George, its worm-eaten and rotten," said the brother.

"Ah," replied the other, "it will do me my lifetime, I'm going to put it in."

To which came the curt reply, "you'll be dead the night then."

125. IF I MAY SUGGEST

The story is told of a young Newfoundland chap who left in his car for Toronto. When passing through Nova Scotia he was stopped by the R.C.M.P. on a routine check. The Mountie asked the young man for his identification and license. As the Mountie was examining the I.D. the mosquitoes began to bother him. The young Newfoundlander noticed the flies and commented, "circle flies bothering you, sir?"

The Mountie not knowing what to make of the comment replied, "what do you mean by circle-flies? These are called mosquitoes."

"Well sir," replied the young Newfoundlander, "circle flies are the flies that circle around the rear end of a horse."

The Mountie thought for a moment and looking at the young man said, "you are not insinuating that I'm a horse's you know what?"

To which the young man replied, "sir, I wouldn't think of suggesting such a thing, but you can't fool those circle-flies."

126. AN HONEST ERROR

In some of the more isolated outports the members of the community were obliged to meet their needs out of their own resources. In life and death there was always a strong sense of togetherness and mutual help. When someone died members of the community would rally around and look after every detail of the funeral.

Out of this isolation customs grew up that varied from region to region. An interesting story is told about a funeral which took place at La Poile some years ago. As was the custom at La Poile a pine box was built and whereas flowers were seldom available the relatives and friends expressed their sympathy and affection for the deceased by placing a sympathy card on top of the coffin. This card was usually attached to the coffin top by a thumb tack which kept it in place and allowed the coffin to be carried to the cemetary without the cards blowing off. The thumb tack was always placed on the inside of the card so that the card could be opened and read without being removed.

As in many places in outport Newfoundland a few years ago some of the residents could not read or write, and in situations like this they often got a friend to help in making the appropriate selection of a suitable card, or took a chance on recognizing the appropriate illustration or symbol.

On this occasion the funeral service was held in mid-summer. It was a beautiful day with a pleasant breeze blowing off the ocean. The mourners gathered in the little cemetary situated near the water's edge. The minister read the commital service and reaching down to pick up a handful of earth he noticed one of the cards on the coffin had blown open in the breeze, and printed on the inside were the words, "Wishing you a Merry Christmas and a Happy New Year!"

127. NO REST FOR THE TOURIST

Stopping at a service station in central Newfoundland on her way through to St. John's the lady tourist inquired of the gas attendant, "do you have a rest room?"

"No, ma'am," replied the attendant, "when any of us gets tired, we keel out on those oil drums over there."

128. NOW HERE'S ADVICE

All the villages have their local philosopher, and some of the wisdom imparted is worth the listening. As is this piece of advice, "If you get up earlier in the morning than your neighbour, and work harder, and scheme more, and stick to your job more closely, and stay up later planning how to make more money than your neighbour, and burn the midnight oil more, planning how to get ahead of him while he's snoozing, not only will you leave more money when you die than he will, but you'll leave it much sooner."

129. CHAULK TALK

Walter Simms tells a story of a well known sea captain from Burgeo who had no formal education. In fact the captain could neither read nor write yet he commanded a vessel around world.

In the early days of telegraph a blackboard was placed outside the telegraph office and the operator would at intervals during the day report the whereabouts of the coastal boat. One afternoon the captain was standing in front of the blackboard along with a group of other citizens when the local merchant happened along. Knowing the captain could not read the merchant thought he might get a laugh at the captain's expense by asking:

"What's on the board today, captain?"

"Chaulk", came the terse reply.

130. THOSE VOICES

A psychiatrist was testing a group of Newfoundland recruits for the army. One young man was being interviewed and during the questioning was asked:

"Do you ever hear voices without being able to tell who is speaking or where the voices come from?"

"Yes, sir, as a matter of fact I do," replied the young man.

"And when does this occur?" prompted the psychiatrist.

"When I answer the telephone," said the young man.

131. A TALL TALE

The story is told of an American Tourist who came to Twillingate and while there became interested in collecting folklore about the place. Walking over the road one afternoon he met Uncle Mose, an eighty year old resident, leaning on his gate. Approaching Uncle Mose, the tourist introduced himself. "Excuse me, but I was wondering if you could tell me some of the old folk tales that are told here in the village. I'm collecting folklore and would appreciate it if you could assist me in this matter."

Uncle Mose sized the gentleman up and said, "you're lookin' fer folk tales eh? Well now me son I don't know too many stories meself, but you see that green house over dere by the hospital? That's me father's place. You go over there and ask him, he'll tell you a good many stories, I'm sure."

"Why don't you come along and introduce me to your Dad?" said the visitor.

"I can't do that," said Uncle Mose.

"Why not?" the tourist asked.

"Well," said Uncle Mose, "the old man owes me a lickin' so I'm givin' him a wide berth."

"But why does your father want to spank you? You're a grown man," the tourist stated.

"Because he caught me throwing rocks at me grandfather," said Uncle Mose with a grin.

132. TAKE NOTE

Since confederation it has been compulsory for children under the age of fifteen to attend school regularly. If a child missed school he was suppose to bring a note to the teacher indicating the reason why he was absent. If you did not bring a note from your parents you were sent home to get one. Some of the notes received were full of innocent humour like the one brought by little Tommy:

Dear Teacher:

'Please excuse Tommy for being away yesterday. He got wet in the a.m. and had to be dried in the p.m.'

133. DREE

The Newfoundlander was being shown the wonders of Niagara Falls. "It took about five million years for this magnificant falls to be shaped like this," explained the guide.

"Another DREE project, I suspect," said the Newfoundlander.

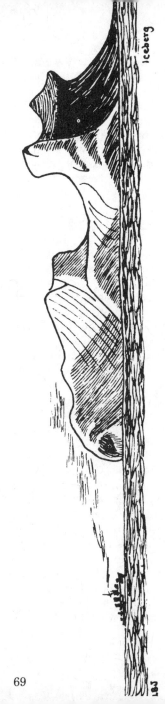

Iceberg

134. HIT THE BALL AND . . .

Harry came home at 6 o'clock from the golf course and said to Mary, "My God I had a terrible day at the golf course today. Just terrible!"

"What on earth happened?" Mary inquired, "I thought you enjoyed golfing."

"Not today," said Harry, "my buddie and I started off this morning and when we got to the fourth hole George dropped down dead. After that it was "hit the ball and drag George, hit the ball and drag George, hit the ball and . . ."

135. THE MASTERPIECE

The story is told of a patient at the Waterford Bridge Hospital who at once fancied himself a painter. Up until that time he had rather leaned to the theory that he was John Cabot. But now quite suddenly he decided that he was intended to depict important historical episodes with paint and canvass.

The management catered to his new interest by supplying him with a modest studio and some supplies. After some weeks he announced that he was prepared to hold a private unveiling of his first masterpiece. He invited the superintendent of the hospital to be his chief guest on the occasion.

At the appointed moment he brought forth a large frame shrouded in cloth. Having placed it where the light would bring out the best values of the composition, he removed the cover with a flourish. There was revealed a stretch of canvass untouched by so much as a single brush stroke.

"Now," said the artist, with pride in his voice, "what do you think of that for a beginning?"

"Very fine," said the tactful superintendent, "but pardon me, what does it represent?"

"Why, don't you see? That represents the passage of the children of Israel through the Red Sea."

"But where is the Sea?"

"It has been driven back."

"And where are the Israelites?"

"They have crossed over."

"But what about the Egyptians?"

"They haven't arrived yet!"

136. ON THE WAGON

An artist painting in the Codroy Valley had a farmer spectator who admired his work.

"Ah," said the artist, "I suppose you too are a lover of the beauties of nature. Have you seen the golden fingers of dawn spreading across the eastern sky, the red stained, sulphurous islets floating in the lake of fire in the west, the ragged clouds of midnight blotting out the shuddering moon, the northern lights dancing to the tune of nature's music?"

"Not lately," said the farmer, "I've given up drinking for over a year."

137. A FAIR ASSESSMENT

The wino went to see the good doctor at the outpatients clinic at the General Hospital. After examining the derelict the doctor commented:

"I can't quite diagnose your case. I think it must be drink."

"All right doctor," replied the patient, "I'll come back when you sober up."

138. GETTING THE JOB DONE

It was potato planting season and Tom had been caught for speeding and not having the money to pay was sentenced to 10 days in jail. His wife was furious and refused to visit him. Instead she wrote him an accusing letter: "Now that you're in that nice comfortable jail I suppose you expect me to dig the potato garden and plant the potatoes. Well, I'm not going to do it."

The fellow got to thinkin', and asked the jailer for paper and pencil and replied: "Don't you dare dig up that garden. That's where I hid all the money and the guns."

Two days later the wife wrote again: "Somebody at that jail must be reading your mail. The Mounties were here with six men and they dug up the whole potato field. What do I do now?"

Back from the jail came a final note: "Plant the potatoes."

139. FORECASTING

The motion picture company, working on location in the small fishing village, was aided by the very accurate weather predictions made by an old-timer. For three weeks the forecasts had been one hundred per cent correct, but one day the old timer refused to predict the next day's weather.

"Is something wrong?" queried the worried director.

"Yes, me son," said the old-timer, "me radio's broke."

140. OUR SECOND LANGUAGE

The curriculum was under discussion at a faculty meeting at Memorial University. The question was whether a basic English course should be compulsory for all freshmen.

"I think it should," said one professor.

"Why do you suggest that?" asked the dean.

"Well," said the professor, "I think it would be advantageous for our young people to know another language besides their own."

141. STANDING IN LINE

George from Crinkle Cove was up for discharge from the army.

The tough army Sargeant said, "well George, I suppose when you get back on civy street you'll hardly be able to wait to come back and punch me in the nose?"

"Not me, Sarge," replied George, "when I get out of the army I'm never going to stand in line again."

142. IT'S THE WAY THEY SPEAK

The Newfoundlander went to Boston to see his relatives. While there he was being shown around by some American friends of the family. Coming to a large statue of George Washington he asked his American friend who it was.

"That, Sir, is a statue of George Washington, first President of the United States. When he was president not a lie passed through his lips."

The Newfoundlander replied, "is that a fact? Then he must have talked through his nose, like the rest of you!"

143. BETTER LUCK

An inebriated fellow was staggering home one night after consuming a fair portion of Newfie Screech when he was knocked down by a bus.

He picked himself up, staggered right back into the traffic, and was immediately hit by a motor bike. He got to his feet and began to complain. The fellow on the bike said: "It's your own fault. You should have walked down the sidewalk and crossed the street where there's a Zebra crossing."

The drunk replied, "Is that so? Well, I hope the Zebra is having better luck getting across the street than I am."

144. BORE ISLAND LIGHT

The captain sent a man on the bow to look out for Boar Island light at the entrance to Burgeo harbour. After a few anxious moments the captain called to the watchman, "do you see the light?"

To which he replied, "yes sir, it flashes two red and one black."

145. ROOM FOR ONE MORE

The minister in the small outport community was visiting a rather truant member of his congregation and in the course of the conversation asked why he did not attend church.

"I don't go to church," he replied frankly, "because there are so many hypocrates there."

"Ah," said the minister, "don't let that bother you. There is always room for one more."

146. A CLOSE CALL

The three Newfoundlanders were sitting together in the popular Toronto evangelical church when the minister announced:

"I want everyone here to put twenty dollars in the collection plate this morning."

One of the chaps fainted, and the other two quickly carried him out. A close call indeed.

147. THE LONG ARM OF THE LAW

Carbonear was one of the towns that had a policeman in pre-confederation days. One constable who served was disliked by the whole community and the basis of this dislike was the fact that he went beyond the call of duty to implicate the residents in some legal issue or other. His boast was that nearly everyone in the town had received a summons from his devotion to duty.

During his tenure as policeman a clergyman was appointed to the Methodist Church to whom he quickly took a strong dislike. He tried without success on a number of occasions to issue the clergyman with a summons. However one day he hit upon a plan that would give him his revenge. Positioning himself at the bottom of Harbour Rock Hill behind a store, he waited for the clergy to cycle down. (Bikes were used in those pre-confederation days.) When the clergyman was about a yard away, the constable stepped out in front of him, thinking to himself, "He'll run over me. It will hurt, but I'll get him for not having adequate brakes."

The minister's reflexes, however, enabled him to stop his bicycle about a foot in front of the burly policeman. The constable reluctantly admitted defeat and said:

"I thought I had you that time, parson."

The minister replied, "ah yes, but God was with me."

"Then I got ya!" said the officer, "two on the one bike."

148. WATER LOGGED

An unconscious man was washed up on a crowded beach near St. John's. The kiss of life and artificial respiration had no effect and an ambulance was summoned to the scene. Upon arrival the attendant, sizing up the situation, decided to apply a stomach pump to the unfortunate victim. To his amazement the pump dredged up several gallons of sea water, a crab, seaweed, and a couple of clam shells. There seemed to be no end to it. The attendant was wondering what to do next when an onlooker said:

"Hey, sir, do you think you ought to be using that pump while he's still sitting in the water?"

149. A STRAIGHT ANSWER

The minister was standing at the door of the church shaking hands with the members of his flock when old Mrs. Brown approached him. The minister taking her by the hand greeted her with the words, "it gives me great joy, Mrs. Brown, to see you always in your pew on the Sabbath day."

To which she enthusiastically replied, "indeed, sir, I'm real glad to come, for its not often I get such a comfortable seat and so little to think about!"

150. DEAD WRONG

The Newfoundlander was up before the courts for stealing a car.

Judge: "You are accused of stealing a car. How do you plead?"

Defendant: "Not guilty".

Judge: "Why do you plead not guilty? You took the car, didn't you?"

Defendant: "Well, your honour, it was like this. I saw the car parked outside the cemetary, and I thought the owner was dead."

Near Hopedale
Labrador

LBJ

151. IN PRAISE OF CHIVALRY

The rather heavy set lady squeezed her way onto the crowded downtown bus, amid the standing room only crowd that hung from the safety straps overhead. Sitting on a front seat close to her was a rather timid looking gentleman who on three occasions attempted to rise but was pushed back into his seat by the same lady who on the third shove said, "look sir, none of this old fashioned gallantry for me. I'm a liberated woman and I can stand as well as the next one."

On the fourth attempt the gentleman thrust out his jaw and said firmly: "For God's sake woman let me off the bus. I'm seven blocks past my stop now."

152. THE WRONG PITCH

The insurance salesman was making a gallant effort to sell life insurance to the outport fisherman. After explaining the benefits of the policy and still noting some skepticism in the eye of the wary fisherman, asked, "how would your wife carry on if you should die?"

"Well," answered the fisherman with some down to earth philosophic reasoning, "I don't suppose that's any concern of mine — as long as she behaves herself while I'm alive."

153. USING TACT

The old fisherman was a cantankerous old cuss but he had a lovely daughter who was engaged to a fine young man from the next cove. When it came time to make plans for the wedding the old fellow got wind of it and insisted that the young fellow come and ask for his daughter's hand in the traditional manner.

To avoid any problems the young man arrived at the house to ask formally for his daughter's hand in marriage. The old fellow knew what he had come for and began the conversation:

"So you want to become my son-in-law, eh?" snarled the old fellow.

"Not exactly, skipper," said the witty young fellow, "but I see no way around it if I am to marry your daughter."

154. PLACING THE BLAME

A professor at Memorial came to class a little late one morning and found a most uncomplimentary caricature of himself drawn on the blackboard. Turning to the student nearest him he angrily inquired:

"Do you know who is responsible for this atrocity?"

"No, sir, I don't," replied the student, "but I strongly suspect his parents."

155. FINDING YOUR WAY

Many Newfoundlanders went to Boston during the Depression in the 1930's to earn a living for their families. For most coming to the big city of Boston from the little villages and towns in Newfoundland was quite an experience. It took some years to learn their way around the city because of its maze of twisting roads and streets.

One Newfoundlander who returned home for a holiday was asked by a friend if Boston was as bad to get around as people said it was.

"I'll say it is," said the returnee from Boston, "why, when I went there first I couldn't find my way around at all."

"That must be bothersome," the friend commented.

"Bothersome? I tell the world it was bothersome. Why, the second week after we got there the wife wanted me to get rid of an old cat that had been left behind in the apartment by the people who lived there before. So I put the cat in a brin bag and carried it clear over to the other side of the city and let it go."

"Well, I guess you got rid of the cat alright?" said the listener.

"Got rid of the cat? Nothing doing. Say, listen, I'd never would have found me way back home again if I hadn't followed that cat."

156. CAME TO SEE ME OFF

The Three gentlemen arrived at the train station and enquired when the train was due in. The Station Agent advised that the train was 20 minutes late. One of the chaps suggested that they had time to go across the tracks to the tavern and have a 'chug a lug a dominion.' This they did and about 15 minutes later arrived back at the station only to learn that a further delay of 20 minutes was in store. So back across the tracks the three went to consume another couple of pints. On arriving back at the station they were again advised that the train was not due at the stop for another 15 minutes. (Is it any wonder that people were drunk on the Newfie Bullet?)

By this time they were in a party mood and didn't seem to care if the train arrived or not. However, they decided to make one more trip across the track. While they were guzzling down their beer the train whistle blasted and the train pulled into the station.

The train, running late, made only a whistle stop at the train station so the three had to run in order to get on. As the train was pulling out of the station the first chap managed to grab the railing on the caboose, and shouting some encouragement to the other two, extended his hand to his nearest companion who managed to make it on board the caboose with him. The third chap, however, feeling the effects of his beer failed to reach the extended hands of his two companions leaning over the rail of the caboose, and could only watch in vain as the lights of the Newfie Bullet faded into the night.

Looking up he saw the station agent standing on the platform. "You see those two fools hanging out of the caboose," he cried, "they came to see me off."

157. FIRST IMPRESSIONS

George, who had been married a considerable number of years, sought the counsel of an officer associate. He confessed that his domestic affairs were slipping into a rut, his wife was getting bored, and there didn't seem to be any romance in their married life. He wanted to know where he went wrong.

His confidant asked if he still paid his wife those little attentions that you used to pay her when you were courting her. "Well," confessed George, "I can't say that I do."

"I thought so," said the wise counselor, "why don't you begin paying your wife a little attention. Fuss over her just as you used to do when you were engaged. Try to be a sweetheart to her as well as a husband."

"Now maybe you're right," said George, "I'll give it a try."

That evening he burst into the front door his arms laden with parcels, he planted a warm kiss upon her lips and in tones of a well worked-up enthusiasm he whispered, "Honey, this is going to be the biggest night of your life! Accept these flowers as a token of our love, and the chocolates as the sweetness of our togetherness. And get yourself together, I'm taking you out for dinner tonight. Why — what's the matter?" he added, as he noticed her lips trembling.

"Well, to begin with," she said, "your aunt Mabel arrived unexpectedly and there's no telling how long she'll stay; the furnace quit about three o'clock; the two children were sent home from school sick and now" — she burst into tears — "and now, to cap it all off you come home drunk!"

158. NOT THAT HANDY

Most Newfoundlanders are pretty handy with the hammer and saw. Harry was out one evening in the yard sawing and hammering away when the neighbour came over. During the course of the conversation Harry mentioned that the wife was pretty sick.

"Is that her coughin'?" asked the neighbour.

"No bye," said Harry, "that's a little go-cart I'm making for the young feller."

159. WHAT KIND OF BIRD

The two Americans from the Argentia Naval Base were hand gliding on the cliffs overlooking Placentia Bay when one of them looked down and saw a couple of Newfoundlanders hiding in a blind waiting for sea ducks to fly pass. "Let's glide down near those two Newfs," said one, "and frighten the daylights out of them."

"Good idea," said the other.

The first hopped off the cliff and began to glide in the direction of the two early morning hunters. Looking up George saw this strange looking object flying towards them. "What kind of a bird is that, Sim?" said George.

"I don't know, bye" said Sim, "but let's put up and give it to her."

The two fired their twelve gauge shotguns. Taking the guns from their shoulder George said, "what in the name of fortune was it?"

"I couldn't say," said Sim, "but whatever it was it wasn't long letting go of that feller it was carryin'."

The "Narrows"
Old St. Johns

160. COMING UP WITH THE RIGHT ANSWER

The magistrate was presiding over an interesting automobile accident insurance case that involved a car and a horse and cart on one of the local roads. The driver of the horse and cart was suing for damages and was being questioned by the defendant's lawyer.

"Did you or did you not say at the time of the accident that you were not hurt?"

"I did, sir," replied the plaintiff, "but you see it was like this. I was driving along the road with me harse and cart when along comes this feller and knocks us into the ditch. There I was flat on me back with me legs in the air, and there was me old harse flat on his back with his legs in the air. Well, sir, this feller gets out of his car and comes over on the bank and takes a good look at us. He sees that the harse has a broken leg so he goes back to the car gets a gun and shoots me harse. Then he turns to me lying there in the ditch and says, 'now, what about you? Are you hurt?'"

161. NOW ABOUT ME PENSION

The elderly lady from Joe Batt's Arm journeyed to Fogo Hospital to see if she could get something to dispel her nervousness.

The doctor after examining the poor soul recommended a series of treatments for her nervous condition and as a word of encouragement he told her, "In a few weeks you'll be 10 years younger!"

"Oh, dear," moaned the poor old soul, "it won't affect my pension, will it?"

162. GONE HOME

The woman was consulting a tombstone dealer with regard to a memorial for her late husband.

"How would a simple 'Gone Home' do?" asked the dealer.

"Perfect," said the widow. "it was always the last place he ever thought of going."

163. APPROPRIATE ADVICE

Newfoundland, we are happy to say, has the lowest divorce rate in Canada and the happiest and closest family life in all of North America. There are occasions, however, when problems arise in families but they are usually handled with that up front sensible Newfie approach that has kept families together and divorce at a minimum. Take this story of Harry and Margaret as an example. Harry went to work one morning and in conversation with a companion mentioned that Margaret was asserting herself and he felt henpecked. The companion advised that a little self assertion was needed in this situation in order to gain mastery of his own home. And appropriate advice was given.

Harry went home that evening and arriving at the front door shouted, "what time is supper?"

"Seven-thirty, like always," answered Margaret.

"Nothing doing," said Harry, "tonight, it's seven sharp. And I want steak instead of that boiled dinner. And when you're finished with supper press my pants. I'm going out with the boys at the office and maybe, just maybe, I might take that little blonde at the office out for a dance."

Margaret froze with astonishment as her husband continued, "and when I'm ready to have my tie fixed in a neat little knot, do you know who's going to tie it?"

By this time Margaret had recovered her voice, "I certainly do," she announced grimly, "the man at Carnell's Funeral Home."

164. DO IT TO ME ONE MORE TIME

The Big Six in St. John's was having one of its Annual Sales and on the opening day of the sale a large crowd of bargain hunters had gathered outside waiting for the store to open. Among them were the usual number of rather vocal and burly ladies. As the time drew near for the doors to open there was some jockeying for position. In the shuffle a rather slight little man began to work his way toward the door but was rebuffed by the women in front of him. He made a second attempt only to be pushed off the curb into the street. Picking himself up he started back toward the door more determined than ever. By this time some of the more vocal ladies were in a surly mood and were about to pick him up physically and toss him back into the traffic when he spoke up: "You do that to me once more and so help me I won't open the store today".

165. THE PILGRIM'S PROGRESS

Some of the best wits in Newfoundland have been clergymen, and it is not uncommon to find the occasional half-wit among them. This story, however, shows the Newfoundland wit at its best. A minister was asking one of his flock why he had not attended church lately.

"Well, you see, sir," said the man, "I'm troubled with a bunion on my big toe."

"Strange," said the minister, "that a bunion should impede the pilgrim's progress."

166. HOW TO KEEP IT NEW

Sam Short always dressed very well and most of the compliments he received were well deserved. One day at the lodge one of his friends commented, "that's a fine hat you got there, Sam."

"Yes bye," replied Sam, "bought it five years ago, had it cleaned three times, changed it twice at church, and three times in restaurants — and it's still as good as new."

167. REACHING THE QUOTA

Sandy got a boarding house in St. John's where he was obliged to pay fifteen dollars a week. One day his landlady said, "Mr. Clark, I'm afraid I'll have to charge you a couple of dollars a week more, you are such a good eater."

"For goodness sake," complained Sandy, "don't do that. I'm killing meself already trying to eat fifteen dollars worth."

168. SOME HELPFUL ADVICE

Two residents of the North Shore met one day in Carbonear.

"Say", queried the first, "what did you give your horse when he had the neaves?"

"Turpentine", offered the other helpfully.

Two weeks later they met again.

"What did you say you gave your horse when he was sick?" asked the first.

"Turpentine", answered the helpful one.

"Well, I gave it to mine and it killed him."

"Killed mine too," said his companion.

169. "NOW TAKE MY BROTHER..."

The visitor watched the Newfoundlander out on the frozen pond sawing ice with a large two man cross-cut saw. He was amazed at the ease in which the saw cut through the ice and admired the strength and toughness of the chap as he went about his work in the bitter cold.

Walking out to where the chap was he said, "I've been watching you cut ice out here in the bitter cold. I must say you are a tough man to be able to stand up to this."

"Naw," replied the chap, "I'm not very tough. Now take my brother he's the tough one! If you're talking about tough, he's tough."

"Well, where is your brother? asked the visitor inquisitively.

"Oh," replied the chap, "he's on the other end of the saw under the ice."

170. RECOGNIZING THE VISITOR

The two relatives had gone to Gander Airport to welcome back a cousin who had been away for twenty-five years. During his long sojourn in the States he had neglected to write home or send a picture of himself.

Said one of the relatives to the other, "how are we going to tell what Angus looks like, we haven't seen him in twenty-five years? I really don't know who to look for when the passengers get off the plane."

"Do you suppose," said the other, "he'll recognize us?"

"He should," said the relative, "we haven't gone away anywhere."

171. WHERE ARE YOU CALLING FROM

A gentleman in St. John's arose one morning and as was his custom began his breakfast with the morning paper. Turning to the obituaries he received the shock of his life when he read his own obituary, apparently placed there by someone with a macabre sense of humour. Dismayed and upset he called his minister who was a personal friend: "George," he began, "have you read the paper this morning?"

"Yes", replied the clergy, "I did glance over it. Why?"

"Did you see my obituary listed there?" went on the exasperated parishoner.

"No I didn't," said the minister, and then hesitantly he asked, "by the way where are you calling from?"

Mickey —
a Newfoundland Dog

L.B.J.

85

172. HUM A FEW BARS

The Newfoundlander was playing his accordian in his apartment in Toronto to the delight of his buddies well into the night when the door burst open and an enraged landlord entered the room yanked the instrument from his hands, and roared: "Do you know there's a little old lady sick upstairs?"

"I don't think I do," admitted the accordian player. "Would you mind humming the first few bars and I'll see if I can pick it up?"

173. AIN'T THAT SOMETHING

The two old fellows from around the Bay were in the city on holiday when a friend suggested that they go and take in a burlesque show just for a bit of excitement. During one of the acts a curvacious blonde was shown taking a bath in a large wooden tub.

"Ain't that something?" said one to his companion.

"Sure is," said the other, "been years since I've seen a wooden puncheon tub like that."

174. THE CALL

Not everyone who wishes to become a preacher is cut out for the job. This apparently was the case with one young man who apparently lacked some of the gifts necessary for proclaiming the good word. One Sunday morning he preached at his home church before the critical eyes of relatives and friends. He was nervous, and, of course, realized that a "Prophet was without honour in his own town and among his own people," but he wanted to make an impression. After the service one old aunt who had sat critically through the service called the young preacher aside and said, "George, why did you enter the ministry?" To which George replied, "Auntie, I had a call."

"You sure," she said, "it wasn't some other noise you heard."

175. WITH THEE ALL NIGHT

After services or prayer meetings were very popular in Newfoundland especially in the outports where Methodism, despite union with the United Church of Canada, was still strong. The after service was a time for personal testimony and prayer. Anyone in the congregation could get up, make a personal witness, offer a prayer, or lead in the singing of a chorus or two.

These meetings were often accompanied with a great deal of emotional outbursts. Handclapping and shouts of 'praise the Lord', 'Amen', and 'hallelugah', were an essential part of the after service.

In some of the more fundamentalist communities these meetings went on well into the morning. At other places the after service lost its appeal and was only attended by those older people who felt the need. Because of this there grew up a custom where you would have the regular service and if anyone wanted a prayer service they could remain afterwards. In most places most of the congregation would leave after the regular service. However, customs die hard in Newfoundland and there would always be the few who would stay for a prayer meeting, and very often the clergy, whether he liked it or not, would have to oblige. Such was the case in one small outport church when the minister announced that after the close of the regular service there would be a prayer meeting. Anyone wishing to remain may do so. In this instance everyone left with the exception of one little old lady who sat in the middle of the church. The minister thought to himself that it had been better if the old lady had left with the others, but seeing she was there the service must go on. Without too much forethought he picked up the hymnary and announced that they would sing a couple of verses of hymn 312.

'Come, O Thou Traveller unknown
Whom still I hold but cannot see;
My company before is gone,
And I am left alone with Thee;
With Thee all night I mean to stay,
And wrestle till the break of day.'

With this the little old lady jumped to her feet and said, "You ain't wrestling with me all night, sir, I'm getting out of here!"

176. A BIT NERVOUS

Shortly after confederation (1949) the Trinity Bay area became a prominent location for mink farms. The reason for this was that a good supply of mink food was available through the annual "pothead" whale hunt. Every spring the waters of Chapel Arm would turn crimson with the killing of the "pothead" and their carcasses would be sold for mink food.

The mink farms provided furs for the fur industry and very often, in summer, became somewhat of a tourist attraction along with the local fare of fishing villages and wilderness. Some of the visitors often displayed complete ignorance as to the nature of the fur trade — some could not, of course, relate the mass killings of the "pothead" whale and the imminent deaths of all those cute little mink in the making of an expensive and elegant fur coat. In any event this was the case with one lady who visited the farm one afternoon. After looking at the mink she turned to the caretaker and said, "how often do you skin them in a year?"

To which came the quick reply, "only once, Madam, after that they get a bit nervous."

177. AFTER DINNER ORATORS

Probably the best introduction to an after dinner speech begins something like this, "Honoured guests, ladies and gentlemen, I have to catch a plane in twenty minutes." With that the guests will know the approximate length of their pleasure or pain.

Now as most Canadians will testify most Newfoundlanders are excellent orators, and people like Joey Smallwood and John Crosbie have made oratorial reputations for themselves all across Canada. However, there are those whose appearance at the banquet halls as guest speakers leave something to be desired. One such gentleman who was to give a speech before the Lions Club was approached by the chairman and asked, "Do you wish to make your speech now, sir, or shall we let them enjoy themselves a little longer?"

178. GETTING EVEN

The long distance transport driver went into a wayside restaurant and ordered a fish and chips. As he sat to eat his meal three motor cycles screeched to a halt on the parking lot and their owners entered the establishment.

Unfastening their headgear and leather jackets they came over to the driver's table. One of them took his fish and ate it, the other ate his chips, and the third drank his coffee. Without saying a word, the driver left the restaurant, got into his truck and drove away.

The leader of the gang laughed and said, "he wasn't much of a man, was he?"

"No," agreed the restaurant owner, "and he's not much of a driver either — he just flattened out three motor bikes on the parking lot with his transport truck when he pulled out."

179. SHE CHICKENED OUT

The story is told of an old lady pensioner who went to the local supermarket and stole a chicken, placing it under her rather large hat.

When she was checking the other items out she fainted, the hat came off and the chicken rolled unto the floor.

"What do you suppose happened to her," queried the clerk, "do you suppose the cold chicken froze her brain?"

"Naw," replied the other, "I guess she just chickened out."

180. REACHING AGREEMENT

The shop steward was suspected of being in with the management but no one could actually prove it. The time came when a new contract had to be negotiated so the shop steward was rightfully appointed negotiator for the fishermen and plant workers.

After a week or so of negotiating the shop steward called the plant workers together and announced that he had managed to work out an agreement. He began, "after long talks with the management I think that I have secured terms that will enable us to go back to work. However," he went on, "I have had to make some concessions. But I am sure you will agree with me that we have won the day. Accordingly, I have good news and bad news for you. I will give you the bad news first. Due to poor markets and all, as a concession to management, I have agreed on your behalf to take a 15¢ cut per hour in your wages. But the good news is that, after strenuous negotiations, the management have agreed to back date the agreement for twelve months."

181. A RETURN VISIT

A bayman who visited St. John's only on occasion was having dinner in one of the down town restaurants when he noticed the manager standing near his table. "Hey, skipper," he said to the manager, "do you remember me?" To which the manager replied, "I can't say that I do."

"Well," said the bayman, "a couple of years ago I came in here to this restaurant and had dinner and I didn't have any money to pay for it, and you kicked me out."

"O yes," said the manager, "now I seem to recall your being here."

"Well," said the bayman, wiping his face with his napkin, "I hate to bother you again, sir."

The mighty Churchill Falls

182. LOOKING AFTER THE REMAINS

The story is told of this Newfoundlander who during the Second World War sought a job in a munitions factory in Toronto.

Replying to questions from the gentleman in the hiring hall he gave his name, age, place of birth, and offered due proof that he had good and sufficient reasons for being exempted from active service himself.

"So far, so good," said the examiner. "Now then, in case of a fatal accident where do you want the remains sent?"

"Where do I want which sent?"inquired the applicant.

"The remains — they would have to be shipped somewhere you know."

The Newfoundlander thought for a minute and edging toward the door replied, "if you don't mind, sir, I'll just take 'em along with me now."

183. MAKING AN EFFORT

One evening when Lige was settled into his favourite chair for a read of the Evening Telegram, his wife, whose thoughts had turned to the morbid consideration of her own demise, interrupted him and asked, 'Lige, if I should die before you do will you promise to keep my grave green?"

"Don't be so foolish," answered Lige, "what's the use of talking about you dying, you're as healthy as a horse."

He went back to his paper. Just as he was about to try and figure out the latest government scandal Hannah interrupted him again. "But Lige, I want to be sure my last resting place will not be neglected. You might get married again or something, and forget me. Dear, are you sure you'll keep my grave green?"

"Hannah," replied Lige, putting down his paper, "I'll keep your grave green supposin' I have to paint it."

184. SOME HOMEY ADVICE

Newfoundlanders had very little need for hotels and motels when visiting around the province. Everyone seemed to have had relatives or friends with whom they were more than welcome. Only on occasion was it necessary for a Newfoundlander in Newfoundland to have to put up in a hotel, and when he did he always considered the cost somewhat high. The story is told of a gentleman who had occasion to visit St. John's and of necessity was obliged to stay in one of the city's hotels. Upon leaving the hotel after paying his bill he spoke with the manager.

"Excuse me," said the gentleman, "but am I right in assuming that you welcome suggestions from guests."

"We do," said the manager, "our constant aim is to increase the efficiency of our service."

"That's reasonable enough," remarked the Newfoundlander, "then I have something to suggest. I've noticed that in your guest rooms, posted where everyone can see, is a small sign which reads 'Have You Left Anything?' I would say that this wording should be altered so that it will read: "Have You Anything Left?""

185. A POOR SCOFFER

Walter Simms in his little book, "A Souvenir of Burgeo — Today and Yesterday," tells about the scoffs that were had in the fall in practically all parts of Newfoundland. Now this 'hot dinner', and it was hot in more ways than one, was usually cooked late at night by a group of young people in their late teens who raided the gardens of their parents or other members of the community for the produce and the hen houses or sheep pens for the meat. The Ballad of "Aunt Martha's Sheep" gives a vivid description of what a scoff really is. There was an art to stealing hens or sheep for the fall scoff and not everyone could bring it off. As was the case with the young man who set out to get a couple of hens one night as his contribution to the evening repasse. Going into the hen house of a rather cantankerous old fisherman he tripped and set the hens a cackling. The old fellow hearing the hens and figuring something was up, pulled on his pants, grabbed the gun, and made his way to the hen house. Standing in front of the door he shouted:

"Who's in there?"

There was a pause and then a quavering voice spoke:

"Tain't nobody in 'ere 'cept us hens."

186. IT PAYS TO ADVERTISE

The local newspaper editor received the following letter from a well meaning correspondent from around the bay.

Dear Sir:

Last Thursday I lost a gold watch which me grandfather had given him for working with the Newfoundland Railway, and I was some upset. The next day a friend of mine told me to advertise the loss of me watch in your paper, and I thought it was worth a try. The very next day after the advertisement was printed, I went home and found the watch in the pocket of me other pants. God bless your newspaper, sir."

187. A GOOD ENOUGH REASON

The disgruntled passenger alighted from the train in Corner Brook and complained bitterly to the conductor about the train being late.

"I can't see why they bother printing timetables for this rail service," he grumbled.

"That's easy enough to figure out, old man," smiled the conductor, "if there was no timetable, you would have no way of knowing how late the train was."

188. A SHORT SHIFT

The gentleman came into the barber shop on Water Street with a small boy, and explained that he had an appointment and would like his hair cut first. This done, he lifted the small boy into the chair, and told him to be a good boy, and to be patient, and then he departed.

When the barber was finished, he lifted the little lad down and sat him in a chair. A half hour passed.

"Don't worry," said the barber, "your dad will be back soon."

The boy looked startled, "he isn't my dad — he just came up to me in the street and said let's both go get a haircut!"

189. ON SCHEDULE

The Newfoundland passenger train had a reputation for not adhering to the printed schedule. Its slow treck across the island had earned it the nickname "the Newfie Bullet."

The story is told of a travelling salesman who used the train extensively to traverse the island selling his wares. One afternoon when he was waiting for the train at Grand Falls he was surprised to see it come in five minutes ahead of schedule. Hailing the conductor he shouted, "Skipper, I want you to accept this cigar with my compliments as a slight token of gratitude."

"What for?" inquired the conductor.

"Because I've been travelling on this train for ten years and this is the first occasion when the train ever got in exactly on time."

"Sir," said the conductor, passing back the cigar to the passenger, "I can't take nothin' on false pretenses. I've got to tell you the truth. This ain't today's train. This is yesterday's train."

190. A CHICKEN SHORT

The merchant who had just one chicken left went into the back of the store to make it appear that he was picking out the best one for the customer. Arriving back he weighed the chicken and said, "well, that comes to $2.54."

Mrs. Curnew said, "well, if you don't mind I would like one just a little bit larger."

So he went back into the back of the store and came back with the same chicken, and said, "that comes to $2.98."

Mrs. Curnew replied, "I believe I will take both of them."

191. UNPLUGGING

Before the plane took off, the flight attendant gave chewing gum to all the passengers. "This will keep your ears from popping when we attain a high altitude," she told them.

After the plane landed in Halifax, a worried man came over to the flight attendant. "This was my first flight," he told her. "It was very nice, but now that it's over, how do you go about getting this gum out of your ears?"

192. GOING FOR HELP

Riding in an old propeller plane across Newfoundland, the passengers saw three of the four engines conk out. The cabin door opened and the Newfoundland pilot appeared with a parachute on his back. Speaking to the passengers he said,

"Keep calm, folks, and don't panic — I'm going for help!"

193. A KNOCK DOWN

After knocking down the woman pedestrian who was jay walking the cab driver stopped and helped the irate lady to her feet.

Refusing his assistance, she shrieked, "you stupid, reckless idiot! You must be blind!

"What do you mean, blind?" snapped the taxi driver, "I hit you, didn't I?"

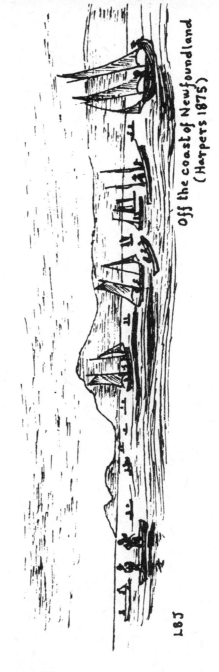

Off the coast of Newfoundland
(Harpers 1875)

LBJ

95

194. LOBSTER POTS

A dear little old lady was visiting the island. One morning she saw the men preparing to go fishing, collecting their pots and nets. She said to one of them: "What are those things?"

The fisherman replied, "lobster pots."

She said, "go on, you'll never train them to sit on those things!"

195. AT THOSE PRICES

The minister was enjoying his tour of the Holy Land. Visiting the Sea of Galilee he asked a local fisherman with a boat if he could take him across the lake.

The fisherman said, "Yes, certainly sir, the charge is fifty American dollars a trip."

The minister replied, "fifty dollars? That's a bit steep isn't it?"

"Well," said the fisherman, "remember our Lord walked across there."

"Yes," said the clergy, "and at those prices I'm not surpised."

196. COOK FOR YOURSELF?

The patient from the bay had been nicely settled in at the hospital and was just beginning to get used to the routine when the nurse came in and opening the door of the bedside cabinet explained to the patient, "here is your bedpan."

To which came the surprised response, "don't tell me you got to cook for yourself in here too?"

197. A GOOD RESPONSE

The Greenpeace fellow wanted to make a protest against the seal hunt. So he covered himself from head to toe in gasoline, put a match to himself — and very quickly died. Just as a protest.

There were big headlines in the papers all across the country. However, everyone in the province collected for his friends and relatives. Up to last night, they had collected 196 gallons of gasoline.

198. CHIPPING IN

The Newfoundlander was up in court for not paying maintenance to his wife. The magistrate said, "you should be ashamed of yourself, Mr. Parsons. I'm awarding your wife one hundred and fifty dollars a week."

Parsons replied, "that's very good of you, sir, and I'll try to send her a few dollars meself."

199. EXTRA CURRICULA ACTIVITIES

One morning the wife of an office worker in St. John's told her husband it was time that he asked for a raise.

"Tell your boss you have twelve children to feed, clothe and educate," she advised.

That night the husband came home looking rather down in the mouth.

"Did you get the raise?" asked the impatient wife.

"No I didn't" said the husband, "in fact I got fired."

"But why? He can't fire you for asking for a raise," insisted the wife.

"No," he explained, "but my boss said I have too many outside activities."

200. A LONG WAY FROM HOME

The Newfoundlander was visiting Texas on some oil business and was being driven by a rancher over a blistering stretch of Texas plains when a large brightly coloured bird scurried across the road in front of them. The visitor asked what it was.

"That's a bird of paradise," said the rancher.

"She's a pretty long way from home, ain't she?" remarked the Newfoundlander.

201. ALL OF A SUDDEN

"What's the matter with you?" the wife demanded. "Monday you liked beans; Tuesday you liked beans; Wednesday you liked beans; now Thursday, all of a sudden, you don't like beans."

202. SUPPORTING THE DAUGHTER

The father was concerned that the young man who was about to marry his daughter may not be able to support a family. So when he arrived at the house the father approached the prospective son-in-law and asked: "Harry, could you support a family?"

"No sir," replied Harry, "I was only planning to support your daughter. The rest of you will have to take care of yourselves."

203. MAKING THE RIGHT MOVES

The first salmon of the season was usually given to the Parish Priest. This was done in the hope that the priest would bless the efforts of the fishermen and hopefully prosper the fishery. Young Patrick was out with his father to haul the salmon nets on the first day of the season and when they landed their catch his father gave him a salmon to take over to the Glebe House for the good father. Arriving at the Glebe House he knocked at the back door. The servant girl answered the knock. "Is Father Pippy in?" said young Patrick.

"Yes he is," replied the young lady. And before she could say anymore young Pat ducked under her arm and came into the dining room where the good Father was having breakfast.

Seeing the boy and figuring out what had happened at the door he decided to teach young Pat a lesson in manners. The priest said, "young man, when you knock at the door of the Glebe House you should wait to be invited inside. Further, you should ask permission to see me." Getting up from the table and taking the salmon he said to the boy, "now you sit down and pretend you are the priest. I'll pretend that I am you, and I will show you how you should behave in this instance." So taking the salmon he went to the door and knocked. The girl answered and he said, "I have a salmon for the father, may I present it to him?" She said, "I will ask permission". So pretending that she had received permission she said, "come this way, please." Entering the dining room the priest said, "Father, here is a salmon that my dad sent over to you. Will you kindly accept?"

The boy acting the part of the priest replied to the surprise of the father, "thank you son, here's fifty cents. Give the salmon to the maid and come and sit down and have a bite of breakfast."

204. MAKING DO

The two old folk were spry for 97 and 95, and were terribly independent. One day, Mrs. Clark was down in the bottom of the garden cutting a cabbage for dinner. But she suddenly fainted and went out like a light. There she was, keeled right out.

Mr. Clark came dashing out, and struggled to pick her up. A next door neighbour who saw the incident rushed over and asked, "can I be of any assistance."

"No, that's all right, " said Mr. Clark, "I'll manage. I'll open a tin of beans."

205. STRIKING A BARGAIN

The Newfoundlander went to the junk yard to get a door for his old car.

"Have you got a door for a 1970 chevelle?" he asked.

"Yes," replied the dealer, "as a matter of fact we have."

"How much?" said the purchaser.

"Oh, it will cost you fifty dollars," said the dealer.

"Fifty dollars! I can get a door up the road for twenty-five!" protested the purchaser.

"Well," said the dealer, "if you can get one up the road for twenty-five dollars why don't you go up the road and get one?"

"Because they haven't got any left," said the purchaser, "they've sold out."

"Well," said the dealer, "when we've got none ours are only twenty-five dollars too."

"Thank you very much, sir," said the Newfoundlander. "I'll come back when you've got none."

206. TRY AGAIN

In the heavy fog off the coast a ship had collided with a small inshore fishing boat. No real damage was done, but as the offending ship tried to back off, it banged into the small fishing craft again. The captain of the ship was afraid he might have done some damage with the second blow. "Can you stay afloat?" he shouted through a megaphone, to the floundering victim.

"I guess so," called back the skipper from the fishing boat, "you want to try again?"

"Niagara" broken down off Cape Race, 1943.

LBJ

207. IT WON'T TAKE LONG

Speaking to a large political gathering, Joey was in fine form. He was eloquently demonstrating through the use of repetition and exaggeration what his government had done for the island. At the same time he was being constantly harassed by a particularly cantankerous heckler who yelled out, "go ahead Joey tell 'em all you know! It won't take long!"

Smiling amiably, Joey replied, "I'll tell them all we both know. It won't take any longer."

208. THE DARK HORSE

When Joey was running for the leadership of his party back in the early seventies someone sarcastically suggested to him that he must be the "dark horse" candidate that was in the running. To which Joey replied, "it seems that way as all the rest appear to be Jack Asses."

209. MIND OVER MATTER

A gentleman boarded the "Newfie Bullet" at Corner Brook and took his seat in the day coach section where another gentleman was kneeled out contemplating the rugged scenery of the West Coast. As he settled himself in he noticed in the rack above his head a rather stout, smallish wooden box, heavily tied together with rope, with augur holes bored in the sides and ends of it. His curiousity was immediately aroused as to what could be in the box, and having made his acquaintance with the other passenger began his inquiry as follows:

"Nice day."

"Yep," said the other.

"Goin' fur."

"Grand Falls."

"Grand Falls, hey — live there?"

"No, visiting."

"Tat your box up dere?"

"Yep."

"Got her tied up pretty good."

"Yep."

"Tis a pretty strong box."

"It tis."

"Got holes in it, I see."

"Yep."

"What's the holes fur?"

"Air."

"What you need air fur?"

"So it can breathe."

"So what can breathe?"

"What I got in the box."

"I see — Well, what have you got in the box, old man?"

"A mongoose."

"A what?"

"A mongoose."

"Mongoose, heh?"

"Yep."

"What is a mongoose, skipper?"

"A small East Indian animal."

"Is it tame?"

"Not very."

"Would it bite?"

"Bite the hand right off ya."

"What you want with an animal like tat?"

"Well," said the first passenger, "I'll tell you. A mongoose is an animal that lives on reptiles, snakes, lizards, toads, and that. Now, I've got an uncle in Grand Falls that's got a bad drinking problem, and when he drinks he's bothered by snakes and lizards. He tells me they crawl all over him. I'm taking that mongoose down there to eat those snakes and lizards."

The second passenger thought for a moment, then he replied, "But ain't dem snakes and stuff imaginery?"

"That's right", replied the other, "and so is that mongoose up there in the box."

210. THE GENTLE CRITIC

They were coming home from the church service when Mrs. Clark said to aunt Rachel, "and what did you think of the minister's sermon this morning?"

"Well," said aunt Rachel, "I found three faults with his sermon this morning: firstly, he read it; secondly, he didn't read well; and thirdly; it wasn't worth readin'."

211. A JOB WELL DONE

Mose had spent most of the summer digging a well so that his woman would not have to go a couple of miles to fetch water. One day while he was eating his lunch, the well caved in, which meant many, many extra hours of work.

Hastily looking about and seeing no one, Mose placed his jacket and cap on the edge of the well, then hid in a nearby shed. A neighbour passing by and assuming Mose was at the bottom of the well, raised the alarm and soon a dozen men were frantically engaged in throwing out the dirt. When the job was done, Mose emerged from the shed and thanked his good neighbours for their services.

212. SOME CAN AND SOME CAN'T

Roy Cochrane tells the story of this fellow who was sent to Dorchester. Having arrived and settled in, he joined his cellmate in the lineup for lunch. Standing in line the cellmate called out the number 15 and all the inmates burst into gales of laughter. Someone else back the line called out the number 21, and again everyone laughed.

"Say," said the chap, "why does everyone laugh when someone calls out a number?"

"Oh," said the cellmate, "we got this Newfie joke book and all the stories are numbered, so when we want a laugh we just call a number."

"Is that right?" said the chap. "Where can I get a copy of this book?"

"Well I got one back in the cell," said his mate, "when we go back you can read it."

Getting back to the cell the chap got the joke book and read it from cover to cover, memorizing all the stories and numbers. Next day in the lineup he called out, "30." Not a soul laughed. He tried another number, "28." Still no one laughed.

"How come no one is laughing," he said.

"Well," said his mate, "some fellows can tell a joke and some can't."

213. GETTING THE FACTS

On a bus trip across the island a Pentecostal was reading his Bible.

A gentleman sitting next to him asked, "do you believe every word in the Bible?"

"Why, of course I do?" replied the religious man.

"You mean to say you believe that a whale swallowed Jonah?"

"Yes, sir, I do."

"Come on now," said the gentleman, "you're just putting me on. How could a whale possibly swallow a man and he survive?"

"When I get to heaven," replied the good man, "I'll ask Jonah."

"Now supposin' Jonah isn't in heaven?" said the gentleman.

"Then you'll have to ask him," came the terse reply.

214. CONSTIPATION

One summer at Petites, a small fishing village on the South Coast, a young student minister was sent to conduct services and serve the congregation. He was an affable young man and soon proved to be a pretty good speaker. The people enjoyed his messages and looked forward to the time of worship.

Gaining confidence he announced one morning that he was no longer going to prepare sermons for Sunday worship, but instead would invite topics from the congregation. A topic to be placed on the pulpit every Sunday for his exposition.

This went on for a considerable time, and consistently the young man came up with a good effort, satisfying most of the congregation. However, some of the old saints felt that this approach might lead to carelessness in his future ministry, and it would be in his best interest if a topic were offered that would give him some difficulties. To this end they sought such a topic. One of the men, with an unsaintly gleam in his eye, suggested that the topic for Sunday be "Constipation". The others agreed that this was an excellent idea. And so it was.

Arriving that Sunday morning the young student noted the topic and proceeded with the service. Coming to the sermon he announced: "The topic of my sermon today is "Constipation" and my text is taken from Exodus 19: 'And Moses took two tablets and went up into the mountain'."

215. IT'S THE TIMING

The Tobacco Company had heard of this old fellow in Newfoundland who had smoked their particular brand of tobacco for over seventy-five years.

Having heard that he was still spry for a man of ninety eight they wrote him a letter and asked if he would like to take part in an advertisement giving a testimonial to their tobacco.

The old fellow not comprehending the situation never bothered to write back. So in a few weeks a gentleman and a film crew arrived in the little fishing village to shoot the ad, hoping that the old fellow would consent.

The old chap was apparently more than willing to do the ad and everything went as planned, until the director asked if he could be on the wharf at 7:30 a.m. so as to have the ad filmed against a beautiful eastern sunrise.

"I can't do it, me son," protested the old man.

"But why?" asked the surprised director.

"Well," he said reluctantly, "I don't stop coughing until about noon every day."

216. NICE MARNIN'

Les Stoodley tells this story about Ernie Manuel from Twillingate who accompanied a delegation of government officials to New York to float a Bond Issue.

Ernie, decked out in his bibbed cap and crooked stemmed pipe, followed his pin-striped companions to the Manhatten Tower where they were to meet with some New York businessmen.

Getting on the elevator Ernie greeted everyone with a cheery, "good marnin', nice marnin'."

At every stop to the 38th floor Ernie extended the same greeting to those who got on, "good marnin', nice marnin'."

At every floor he was met with the same cold, silent response.

Getting off at the 38th floor Ernie turned around, removed his crooked stemmed pipe from his mouth, and cupping it in his hand against his chest, announced, "the hell with ya, I still say tis a nice marnin'."

Old St. John's —
a memory

217. SOCK IT TO 'EM

Another of Les Stoodley's favourite stories is about Blanche Cluett, who ran a boarding house in Grand Bank when the town was dry.

Three salesmen from St. John's was staying at Blanche's place and one evening left the boarding house in search of something to drink. They apparently found what they wanted and after having a good night on the town arrived back at Blanche's in the wee hours of the morning completely "ossified."

They commenced to arouse Blanche and after banging on every window and door for about 20 minutes Blanche emerged. Maybe it was to their advantage they were drunk. At 3:00 a.m. Blanche was an encounter of the third kind; her teeth were in a cup upstairs; her hair done up in brown paper curlers; and her sense of humour totally destroyed by the strong smell of liquor on the breaths of the three gentlemen. She was fit to be tied.

Confronting the three gentlemen she cut loose, "a fine pair the three of you make. Comin' home here in the middle of the night, three o'clock in the marnin' with your bellies full of paralized drunk. If you want to stay here you got to find another boardin' house."

With that she closed the door in their face and went back to bed.

218. AN EMPTY TANK

The three candidates running for election had all visited the farmer to get his vote. All of them came when the farmer was milking his cow, and all of them spent a few minutes assisting him with the milking.

However, the next day the farmer couldn't find the politically harassed cow anywhere. Walking over the road he met a neighbour and asked if he had seen the whereabouts of the cow.

"No," replied the good neighbour, "but don't worry she can't get far on an empty tank."

219. THE SUBSTITUTE

The motorist felt obliged to go to the house and advise the lady that he had just killed her rooster that was on the road.

"I'm afraid I killed your rooster Ma'am," he announced, "but I'd very much like to replace him."

"Whatever suits you," said the old lady, "go around to the back and you'll find the hens waiting for you."

220. COMPLAINING

Some people love to complain. In fact they complain so much and so often that they fail to recognize opportunity when it comes their way. As one old fellow put it, "one day fortune actually knocked on this fellow's door. But he did not hear it. He was at his neighbour's house telling a hard luck story."

221. APATHY

"Apathy," said the visiting lecturer, "is the biggest problem in this country."

"What did he say?" said a chap in the back row.

"I don't know, and I don't care," said his companion.

222. A MAJOR CHANGE

The oldest inhabitant of the community was being interviewed and after a number of questions about old age was asked that if he had his life to live over again would there be any major changes that he would make.

He thought about it for a minute.

"Yes, I think I would have made at least one change," he mused.

"Now, sir, what would that be?" said the interviewer.

"Well now, come to think of it, I think I'd part me hair in the middle."

223. CUTTING DOWN

The poor fellow lay dying in the little room just off the kitchen. The family had gathered and sensing the worse began making preparations for the funeral. As he lay there he could hear the family speaking in low tones about the funeral arrangements.

"Well, will we have a couple of cars with the hearse?"

"Why don't we use a station wagon and our own cars and cut out the hearse? It's awfully expensive you know."

"Maybe we should get a couple of family wreaths?"

"Ah, flowers are too expensive, anyway the old man didn't like flowers."

With this the old fellow struggled to a sitting position and shouted as best he could to the family in the kitchen.

"Bring me me pants. I'll walk to the graveyard and save you the bother."

224. FIRST UP

This fellow had spent the night at the Red Rooster tavern in Harbour Grace. He left the place 'paralized' and attempted to find his way home. Taking a short cut across the cemetary he fell into a newly dug grave. Unable to get himself back out, he lay exhausted in the rough box and was soon fast asleep. At eight the next morning he was aroused by the whistle of the local fish plant. He staggered to his feet and looked around.

"Well blessed fortune," he mumbled to himself, "Judgement Day and I'm the first feller up."

225. NO WAY

Aunt Mary Ellen Hiscock, Aunt Nell as she was affectionately known in Victoria would always have an amusing poem or little monologue to offer at the local concert. One of her favourites was a monologue about an old lady who put a mustard plaster on her husband's chest. The laughter came when it was discovered that instead of placing it on his chest she placed it on his 'sea chest' that he took to the Labrador. She was a born entertainer with a wealth of natural ability.

Somewhere in the lines she told of a lady who came and asked how to apply a mustard plaster. After giving the lady advice she inquired a week later, "well did you try the mustard plaster on your husband?"

"Yes I did," came the mournful reply, "but he wouldn't have it. Even when I made it into sandwiches he wouldn't eat it."

226. IN SELF DEFENCE

The Bayman was visiting St. John's when he was attacked by two muggers on Duckworth Street. He put up quite a fight but was eventually subdued and had his wallet lifted from him. The muggers going through the wallet found a one dollar bill and some change.

"Why did you kick up such a fuss for just a buck-fifty?" said one.

"Why," said the Bayman, "I thought you were after the twenty dollars I got in me shoe."

227. SLOW ME DOWN

The foreman on the job had loaded the wheelbarrow sky high with lead pipe.

"Sir," said the Newfoundlander, "would you mind tying a couple of concrete blocks around my ankles?"

"What in the name of fortune for?" asked the foreman.

"So that I won't break into a trot with this load," came the reply.

228. BEHIND SCHEDULE

The passenger got on the Newfie bullet and as the train began to get further and further behind schedule he complained bitterly to the conductor.

"Why don't you get off and walk, old cock?" said the conductor.

"Because I'm not in that big of a hurry," came the quick reply.

229. GET A COUPLE

At the city council meeting one of the councillors suggested that a gondola be introduced to Bowring Park.

The Mayor thought it was an excellent idea and supported it with utmost enthusiasm.

"Let's get a couple, a male and a female."

230. NOW I LAY ME DOWN

I like to tell this story about a friend of mine in Halifax, Jack Kimber. Jack came to church every Sunday, apart from the Sundays that he had to work, and when there he was always a keen critic of the sermon.

The slightest historical error, fact, or wrong date meant that you received, pinned on the door of the study, a note reminding you of the error along with the correct information. It was a lot of fun having Jack in the congregation.

Strangely enough Jack looked as if he was asleep during the sermon. And one day, before I knew how awake he was, he asked me what would be an appropriate prayer to say as a meditation before the service began. I thought for a moment and replied, "for you Jack — Now I lay me down to sleep."

231. A POOR SHOT

Sim got a job at a boarding house in St. John's. He wasn't in the boarding house more than a week when he discovered that the moths were eating his clothes. Going downtown to the hardware store he asked if they had anything for moths.

"Yes," replied the young clerk, "we can give you some mothballs. That should kill them."

Sim purchased a pound of mothballs and left the store.

A couple of days later he came back and asked the clerk for another pound of mothballs.

"But," said the clerk, "didn't I sell you a pound of mothballs a couple of days ago? That was enough for anyone to kill half the moths in St. John's.

"He'd have to be a better shot than I am," replied Sim, "I keep missing the dam things."

232. RALPHOGLYHICS

Anyone visiting the Roy Building on Barrington Street, Halifax, may chance to meet the building's caretaker, Ralph Dawson, known affectionately by the tenants as Ralpho. To the many people who come and go Ralph provides a bit of laughter.

I asked Ralph, sensing his warm humour, if he might not be a Newfoundlander. "Well," said Ralph, "I'm Irish on my mother's side and Scottish on my father's side and I had an operation on my uncle's side." A typical Ralpho answer.

The tenants at the Roy Building find great delight in the messages that Ralpho pins to his door when he has to leave his station to run errands, attend to repairs, or go for lunch. Some of them I'm sure will give you a chuckle.

At holiday time this year the following note was pinned to his door:

"BE BACK IN A MONTH OR SO — PLEASE DON'T WAIT."

Thank you, Ralpho!

Other notes that appeared from time to time had these messages:

"I AM NOT HERE — HAVE GONE TO HAVE MY SHOE LACES LAUNDERED AND PRESSED.

Back 1 O'Clock   Ralpho!

SORRY FOR ABSENCE — TRAINING "PRIVATELY" TO BE AN ASTRONAUT DURING LUNCH BREAK. BE DOWN 1 O'CLOCK.

Ralpho!

IN BOTTOM OF ELEVATOR SHAFT EATIN' DINNER — BE BACK WHEN I FIND A WAY TO GET OUT. HELP!

Ralpho!

GONE TO THE MOON TO COLLECT ROCK SAMPLES. BACK AT 11.

Ralpho!

GONE TO THE ZOO TO VISIT SOME OF MY RELATIVES. BACK IN A BIT.

Ralpho!

GONE TO THE "NUT HOUSE" TO GATHER NUTS FOR THE SQUIRRELS. BACK SHORTLY.

Ralpho!

And this one I think takes the cake.

TO WHOM IT MAY CONCERN

SORRY, BUT I AM NOT HERE. HAD I THOUGHT FOR A MINUTE THAT I WOULD NOT BE HERE NOW, I WOULD HAVE STAYED HERE LONGER. THEN WHEN YOU CALLED I WOULD BE HERE. HOWEVER, IF YOU DID NOT CALL, THEN I WOULD HAVE STAYED HERE ALL MORNING FOR NO GOOD REASON AT ALL. SO I HAVE DECIDED TO LEAVE AND GO TO WHERE I AM NOW, WHICH OBVIOUSLY IS NOT HERE. BUT IS SOMEWHERE ELSE.

Totally confused!   Back 1 o'clock   Ralpho!

Hunting Camp – Grand Pond
(from Capt Kennedy)

L.B.J.

113

233. MOVING UP

A couple moved from the bay to St. John's. In their new surroundings they tried to live up to the snobbish life of the townie. One evening in conversation with some high-brow acquaintances the conversation turned to Winston Churchill, "absolutely brilliant, a fine politician, a great statesman, a genius, Churchill."

The young woman wanting to join the conversation remarked casually, "oh yes, Churchill, a lovely man, a fine person, Why only this morning I saw him get on the number 18 bus going to Mount Pearl."

There was a sudden hush and everyone turned and looked at her. Her husband was shattered. He took her away saying, "Come on Mary, get your coat we are leaving for home."

Driving home the husband kept muttering to himself. Finally his wife turned to him.

"You are mad at me for something."

"Oh really?" You noticed I'm mad?" he said sarcastically. "Well, I'm going to tell you I've never been so embarrassed in my whole life. You saw Churchill get on the number 18 bus to Mount Pearl this morning! You stupid idiot! Don't you know the number 18 bus doesn't go to Mount Pearl?"

234. THE FREE WIT OF THE FREE SPIRIT

Uncle Free came down on the wharf one morning to meet the steamer. A lot of people visited the steamer to meet friends, collect freight or just to talk to the passengers to get the news of the Coast. On this particular morning a good crowd had gathered and among them the superintendent of the highway construction crew that was building the road to Burgeo. Uncle Free wanting a bit of fun went over to the gentleman and began a conversation.

"Nice marnin', skipper."

"Yes," replied the gentleman, "it looks like its going to be a nice day."

"By the way," says Uncle Free, "I don't think you washed your eyes out dis marnin'."

The gentleman taking this comment to mean he hadn't washed his face before coming out to the steamer replied, "I most certainly did wash my eyes out this morning!"

"How come," says uncle Free with a grin, "they're still in your head?"

235. WHAT IN THE WORLD CAME OVER HIM

Uncle Free called the minister's wife one day shortly after the minister had paid him a visit at his home.

"Hello," he said, "I called to tell you that something came over your husband today while he was visiting with me. However, he's alright and has since left to visit another member of his flock."

The poor woman, somewhat alarmed, asked, "what happened? Are you sure he's alright?"

"Oh he's alright," said Uncle Free, "in fact the same thing came over me too."

"What in the name of world was it?" she asked.

"Oh, it was just an aeroplane," smiled Uncle Free.

Needless to say she was mad enough to kill him.

236. IT'S MINE

Uncle Free was always up to his tricks. One day I recall going over to his house and when he answered the door he looked rather sombre.

"What's up Uncle Free?" I said. "You don't look too happy today."

Rubbing his left arm he said, "poor Sarah haven't got the use of this arm today."

Surprised I asked with some concern, "did she have a stroke or something?"

"No,' he said, "she's never had the use of this arm 'cause it's mine."

237. IN THE WHEELHOUSE

Uncle Free was never without a quip or a little trick or something. That's what made him the interesting character that he was. One day I went over to pick him and his friend up in my car to take them to Messers, another part of Burgeo.

Arriving at the house I found the two of them ready. Coming to the car Uncle Free said to his companion, "You get back aft, I'll sit up in the wheelhouse with the skipper."

Telegraph House, Trinity Bay.
As it looked in 1857

L B Jensen
after R Dudley

116

238. GET WELL

The minister had taken ill and was confined to hospital. One of the board members came to visit with him.

"How are you feeling now, reverend?" the member asked.

"Oh, I'm feeling much better thank you," replied the clergy.

The member taking a get-well card from his pocket announced, "we had a committee meeting the other night and they voted to send you this get-well card. The motion passed 4 to 3!"

239. MORE LIGHT

During a meeting of the trustees of the church, one of the members suggested that a chandelier was needed for the Church.

"I don't think that's a very good idea," said an old fellow in the back of the church.

"Why don't you think we need a chandelier? asked the minister.

"Well sir, first of all I don't think there's anyone here that can spell it; and second, there's no body in the church that can play it; and, besides, what this church needs most of all is more light!"

240. HYDRO POWER

The minister was conducting his first service in the small outport church. He brought into the pulpit with him a pitcher of water and a drinking glass. As he preached he drank until the pitcher of water was completely gone.

After the service someone asked an old lady of the congregation what she thought of the new minister.

"He's alright, I suppose?" she replied, "but I must admit he's the first windmill I ever saw that was run on water."

241. CONCERNED NEWF

In collecting this treasury of humour and wit I had one letter that laid down the guidelines as to what the book should be. I hope that I went close to what this colorful correspondent expected in a book of this kind. The letter read as follows:

Well sir,

'I hopes your book on Newfoundland humour is not a pile of those Newfie jokes that they tell on the mainland. If it is you won't sell many of 'em I can tell 'e. Why, getting a laugh out of some of them so called Newfie jokes is like milkin' a buck goat in a sieve. Tis well nigh impossible to laugh at some of those stupid Newfie jokes unless, I suppose, you're a mainlander with nare bit of humour yourself.

Now we all like an odd laugh or two. But bye, I'm tellin' ya, I don't like makin' fun a' people, I don't care where they come from. The radio man the other day was mentionin' about the tourist that come here from the mainland. He said that they were pollutin' the place. Now I don't think that's fair, although the past few summers I've noticed a black ring around the shoreline where they go swimmin'. I don't care if some of them is as oily and greasy as a Tickle-ass we shouldn't make jokes about them.

Now what really gets me dander up is the gall of some people, even our own, to make jokes about the fact that we Newfoundlanders are dirty. I don't suppose there's a cleaner bunch of people on God's green earth. Clean? Me son, I can tell you stories of people on the island that are so clean that just readin' about them would make you go and have a bath just to feel comfortable in their presence, so to speak. Sure, I know a woman right here in the place that is so house proud that she got newspapers under her Cuckoo clock. Not only that she got curtains up to the little window in the oven door. She told me herself it was not just for looks either. She said that being a religious woman she didn't want people looking through the window at the naked chicken. The result, I suppose, of our strict moral upbringing here on the island.

Now, you know yourself that we Newfoundlanders are not stun. What would those fellers do on the mainland if they didn't have a few of us runnin' things for them up there? Be gar, they told I one time that a feller from home had an operation for a

118

brain tumour in Halifax, he comed too to quick when they were operatin' and he took off when his brain was still out of his 'ead. Sure, he was teachin' at that big university in Toronto a couple of years before they discovered it was he. And they got the face to make up jokes about us?

I'll hope you give us some good stories and not that foolish stuff that comes from the mainland. That stuff is worse than the weather they sends our way. That's bad enough. Someone was sayin' the other day we haven't had a case of sun stroke on the island for the past four hundred and fifty years, and we won't have a good laugh either if your book is filled with those Newfie jokes.

I'll be lookin' out fer 'e?"

Concerned Newf.

THE PHONE SONG

Freeman Melbourne

I will sing you a ditty
It's not very long
It's nine or ten verses
'tis called the phone song.
I rhymed it together
The best I knew how
And if you keep quiet
I'll sing it right now.

The phones are in Burgeo
It is a great thing.
The women will run
The minute it rings.
They get on the line
And their yarn is so long
The next thing they know
Their soup is burned on.

The men they don't bother it
Hardly at all
It's only on business
That they make a call.
They talk a few minutes,
Like men always do
And flings down the receiver
As soon as they're through.

Now Mr. Phil Matthews
His badge it does shine
He calls us to know
If the boat is on time.
Yes, she's out of Grand Bruit
And down off Connoire.
She'll dock here in Burgeo
In two hours I'm sure.

Now Mr. Cyril Bowdridge,
He works on that line.
He's been mail man now
For a very long time.
He called us and asked
When the steamer is due,
Uncle Free came right back
"She's coming down through."

The Town Council of Burgeo
Is certainly alright
Most all of the houses
Have got 'lectric lights.
No lamps to be filled
No chimneys to clean,
Just tell the old woman
To tug on the string.

Mr. Jack Mercer
He works for the town.
He climbs on the poles
When the wires come down.
He also reads meters
And tells what you owe.
You pay him the money
And out he will go.

There's one thing here ladies
I'd like to bring in
Just have a lamp filled
And a chimney kept clean.
'c'us there might come a glitter
And bang goes the pole
And you're left in the darkness
And can't see a soul.

The fish plant in Burgeo
Is due some great praise
The thousands of dollars
To people it pays.
They're paid every Thursday
Their money right down
To spend where they like
Right here in the town.

I called Uncle Free
But he never called back
He's probably up
To Connoire in his shack.
If he isn't there
Tis into his mind
To go in the morning
Please God, if it's fine.

Now Oliver Brayon
He goes with him now,
They shape up their course
When they get to the sou'.
They steer up nor'west
To Barachois Point
Call in at Wreck Island
And stay there all night.

Here comes the "Five Brothers"
She's making good speed
They came from Connoire
With a good breeze indeed.
Uncle Free doesn't care
For he knows she's all right.
She's all copper fastened
And that makes her tight.

PROOF READER'S FOOTNOTE

De biggest of aal joaks
In dis book may be
Dat, Joe boy, you lef
The proof-raiding d'me.
Tho me readin' is good
Me writin' is better
Me spellin' is best
But not write to d' letter.

But proof raidin' dis book
Was for me, quite a task.
Why do it at aal?
You may very well ask.
I'd a hunch I was always
D' littery type.
So I says to me self
Bob! d' time might be ripe.

I started of sure dat
I knowed what to do,
But den me book larnin'
Begin d' shine t'rough
An' what wit declensions
An' parsin' and' spellin'
It stumbled me up
In a way ders no tellin'.

I tried all d' rules
But de was no good.
Tho' I took 'em an' 'plied 'em
As best as I could..
So der fer a wile boy
'Twas some awful stew.
Me tryin' me bes'
But not knowin' wat to do.

But den I got t'inkin'
'bout larnin' a bit —
See, som t'ings is larned
From humour an' wit.
Dos' t'ings is like goodness
de' comes from d'heart.
An' dis kind a larnin'
Sets people apart.

Book larnin's no good
If ya can't take a joke
Just as it don't help ya
To love other folk.
Laughin' is sharin'
An' sharin' is givin'
An' das d'best t'ing
Der is about livin'.

So I stumbled at first,
But I still ain't complainin'.
But ders just one small t'ing
Dat I t'ink needs explainin'
So I'm writin' dis down now
So people will no —
"If der's any mistakes,
Don't blame em on Joe."

See, Newfoundland jokes
Is made a mistakes,
An' usually anyt'ing else
Dat it takes.
So wat do I care
When I'm laughin' wit glee,
If the joake is on somebody else
Or on me.

So, now Joe me sun,
Me proof raidin' is t'rough
D' *joakes* was so good
I had nar t'ing t'do.
An' Uncle Free Melbourne
Done sech a good job,
Dat I'll sine off sane,
"What fun it was" — Bob.

P.S.
De calls dis a *foot*-note —
I can't understan;
But, cross me heart Joe, boy
I done 'er be han'.
I don't min' d' note part,
Now das a bit better.
I never intended
To write 'e a letter.

INDEX

(Numbers in Index refer to Story Numbers)